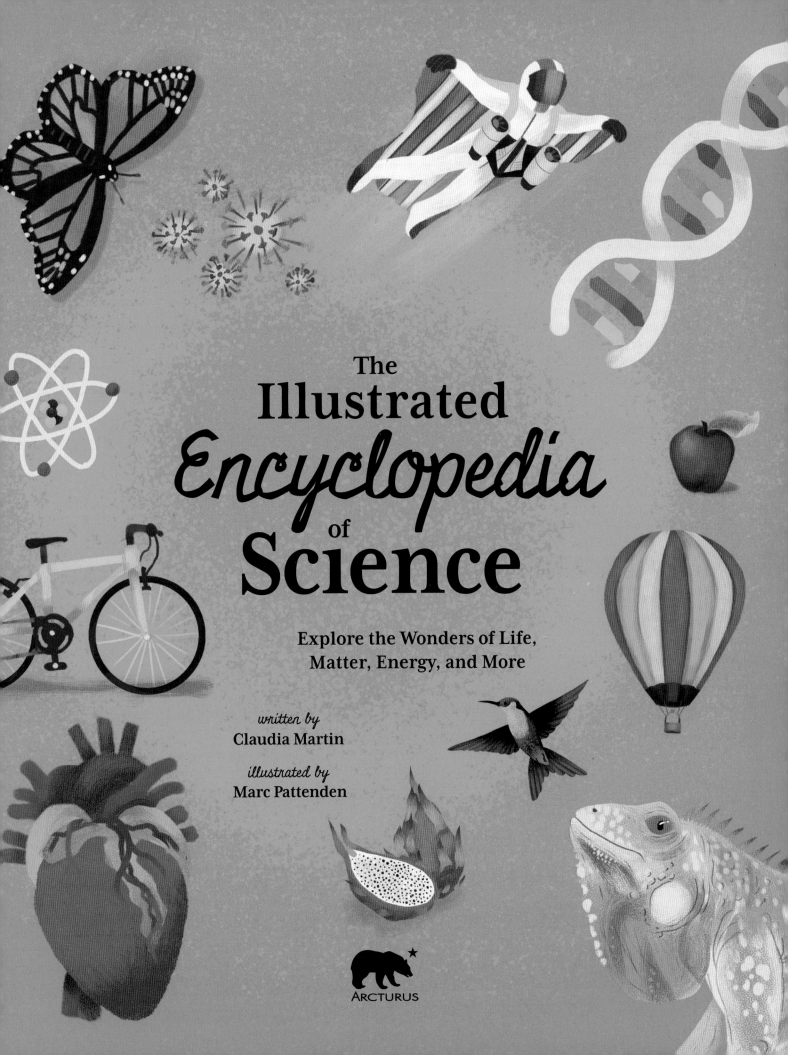

The
Illustrated
Encyclopedia
of
Science

Explore the Wonders of Life, Matter, Energy, and More

written by
Claudia Martin

illustrated by
Marc Pattenden

ARCTURUS

A note on large numbers:

1 million	1,000,000
1 billion	1,000,000,000
1 trillion	1,000,000,000,000
1 quadrillion	1,000,000,000,000,000
1 quintillion	1,000,000,000,000,000,000
1 sextillion	1,000,000,000,000,000,000,000
1 septillion	1,000,000,000,000,000,000,000,000

ARCTURUS

This edition published in 2024 by Arcturus Publishing Limited
26/27 Bickels Yard, 151–153 Bermondsey Street,
London SE1 3HA

Author: Claudia Martin
Illustrator: Marc Pattenden
Designer: Rocket Design (East Anglia) Ltd.
Consultants: Steve Parker, Dr. Kristina Routh, Dr. Sharon Ann Holgate
Editor: Becca Clunes
Design Manager: Rosie Bellwood-Moyler
Editorial Manager: Joe Harris

ISBN: 978-1-3988-4329-5
CH010502US
Supplier 29, Date 0424, Print run 00005687

Printed in China

Contents

Super Science

Science is the study of the world, space, and everything else. Science uses questioning, testing, and watching to build our understanding of how everything works and why. First of all, scientists ask questions, such as: "Why does water flow?", "Why do I breathe?", or "Why can't I put my hand through a table?" Then scientists figure out possible answers, known as theories. Scientists test their theories by carrying out experiments and by watching closely for causes and results. They search for evidence that proves their theories—as well as for evidence that proves their theories are wrong.

We know the answers to those three questions—which you will find in the pages of this book—because of all the scientists, over many centuries, who have questioned, tested, and watched. Those scientists shared what they learned, so that others could build on it. Above all, we know the answers to those questions because scientists dared to ask them in the first place. Rather than simply accepting that, of course, hands cannot plunge through tables—they asked: "Why?" It is by asking questions that anyone, young or old, becomes a scientist.

There are many branches of science. Three of the main ones are chemistry, biology, and physics. Chemistry studies the nature of matter, which is anything— from people to rocks—made of tiny building blocks called atoms. Chemistry studies how atoms join and change. Biology is the study of living things, from dogs to mushrooms. Biology studies how living things feed, move, and grow. Finally, physics is the study of how matter interacts with energy, such as light, heat, or movement. Physics studies why apples fall from trees, why planets orbit—and why hands cannot plunge through tables.

To understand how you make a ball bounce, you need some biology, chemistry, and physics. Biology explains how you move your arm muscles; chemistry shows how the arrangement of the ball's atoms makes it bouncy; and physics explains how high the ball flies.

The chemist Rosalind Franklin (1920–58) helped discover how atoms are arranged in deoxyribonucleic acid (DNA). Found in most living things, DNA holds the instructions for how living things look and function. Franklin's work led to huge breakthroughs in biology.

Matter

Everything you can see or touch is made of matter, from people to plants and paperclips to planets. Matter is anything that has volume and mass. If something has volume, it takes up space. If something has mass, you can weigh it on a scale—as long as you have a scale that is sensitive enough to weigh a speck of matter or big enough to weigh a star!

All matter is made of tiny particles called atoms. The average person is made of 7 octillion atoms—that is a 7 followed by 27 zeros. There are 118 different types of atoms, such as hydrogen atoms and gold atoms. Something that is made of just one type of atom is called an element. Hydrogen and gold are two of the 118 elements. Each element has different characteristics. Hydrogen is a clear gas at room temperature, but gold is a shiny solid.

Atoms can form chemical bonds with each other, joining together to make groups of atoms called molecules. When a molecule contains different types of atoms, it is called a compound. A compound has different characteristics from the elements it contains, which is why you can see and touch many different types of materials with many characteristics, from waterproof to bendy, hard to crumbly. The human body contains more than 20 elements, forming thousands of different compounds. In the whole Universe, there are millions upon millions of different compounds, all made of those 118 different types of atoms.

Oxygen atoms (pictured) make up 65 percent of the human body's mass. Most of those oxygen atoms are joined to two hydrogen atoms, forming the compound known as water. In fact, you contain twice as many hydrogen as oxygen atoms. However, an oxygen atom weighs 16 times more than a hydrogen atom, so oxygen accounts for much more of your mass.

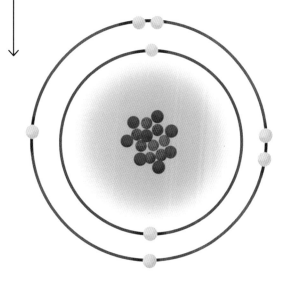

The Polish-French scientist Marie Curie (1867–1934) discovered the elements polonium and radium. These elements are found on Earth only in tiny quantities, in compounds with other elements. Polonium and radium are radioactive (see page 28), which means they give off energy.

Atoms and Molecules

Atoms are the tiny building blocks of all matter. Around 0.0000002 mm (0.000000008 in) across, they are far too small to be seen with the human eye. A group of joined atoms is called a molecule. The smallest molecules have two atoms, while the largest have millions.

ATOMS

An atom is made of even smaller particles. In the middle of an atom is its nucleus, which is made of particles called protons and neutrons. Electrons spin around the nucleus. Electrons have a negative electric charge (see page 92), while protons have a positive charge. Neutrons have no charge. Since atoms usually have an equal number of protons and electrons, these opposite forces normally balance, leaving atoms with no electric charge.

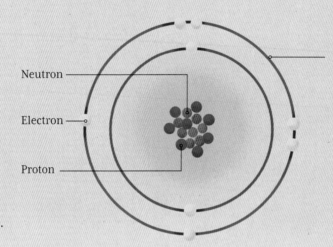

An oxygen atom usually has 8 protons, 8 neutrons, and 8 electrons.

Neutron

Electron

Proton

Electrons spin around the nucleus in layers called shells. Each shell can contain only a certain number of electrons: The first shell can hold up to two electrons, the second shell up to eight, the third shell up to 18, and so on. An oxygen atom usually has 2 electrons in its first shell and 6 in its second shell.

ELEMENTS

There are 118 different types of atoms. Materials that are made of only one type of atom are known as elements, so there are also 118 elements (see page 10). Each type of atom has a different number of protons in its nucleus. An atom of hydrogen has just 1 proton in its nucleus, making it the lightest atom—and hydrogen the lightest element. The heaviest element is oganesson, which has 118 protons in each of its atoms.

A hydrogen atom has 1 proton. It is the only atom that usually has no neutrons. With just 1 electron shell, it is one of the smallest atoms.

An oganesson atom has 118 protons. With 7 electron shells, it is one of the biggest atoms.

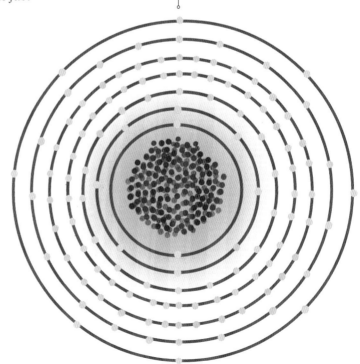

MOLECULES

Molecules form when atoms share or give away electrons, which joins them together. This is known as chemical bonding. Some molecules contain only one type of atom. For example, the oxygen you breathe is made up of molecules with two oxygen atoms (see page 68). Many other molecules contain two or more different types of atoms. These molecules are known as compounds. For example, water is a compound containing oxygen and hydrogen atoms.

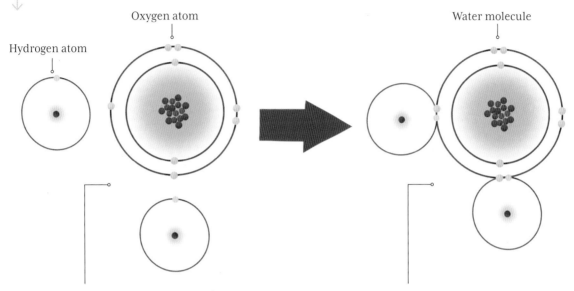

Oxygen atom

Hydrogen atom

Water molecule

Atoms "try" to fill up their outer electron shell. Hydrogen has 1 electron in its only shell, but has room for 2. Oxygen has 6 electrons in its outer shell, but has room for 8.

Two hydrogen atoms share their electron with an oxygen atom, joining the atoms to form a water molecule. This fills the hydrogen atoms' electron shell, with 2 electrons each. It also fills the oxygen atom's outer shell, with 8 electrons.

A compound has different properties from the elements it contains. At room temperature, water is a liquid, but—on their own—oxygen and hydrogen are gases.

Scientist Profile

NAME   John Dalton

DATES   1766–1844

NATIONALITY   British

BREAKTHROUGH

He figured out that each molecule in a compound contains a set number of atoms of each element. For example, we now know that a water molecule always contains one oxygen and two hydrogen atoms, which scientists write as a formula: H_2O, where H is for hydrogen and O is for oxygen.

The Periodic Table

The periodic table displays the 118 elements. Elements are substances that are made of only one type of atom and cannot be broken down into simpler substances. Alone or with each other, the elements form all the materials we can see and touch.

The elements are displayed in order of their number of protons (see page 8), which is known as their atomic number. The table starts at the top left with hydrogen, which has 1 proton and atomic number 1. It ends with oganesson, at bottom right, which has atomic number 118.

The table was devised by Russian scientist Dmitri Mendeleev in 1869. He figured out that when the elements are displayed in this way, elements with similar properties fall into the same columns. He left spaces for the elements he thought must exist but had not yet been discovered.

PERIODS

The table is in seven rows, known as periods, which run across the table. (The two extra rows at the bottom are extensions of periods 6 and 7, because there is not enough room to fit them in the right places.) The elements in period 1 have one electron shell (see page 8), while those in period 2 have two shells ... up to the elements in period 7, which have seven electron shells.

ABBREVIATIONS

Each element is presented with its name and an abbreviation (shortening). Some abbreviations are obvious, such as Sc for scandium, while others are based on the element's Latin or German name, such as Au for gold (short for Latin *aurum*).

1		3	4	5	6	7	8
1 H Hydrogen	2						
3 Li Lithium	**4 Be** Beryllium						
11 Na Sodium	**12 Mg** Magnesium						
19 K Potassium	**20 Ca** Calcium	**21 Sc** Scandium	**22 Ti** Titanium	**23 V** Vanadium	**24 Cr** Chromium	**25 Mn** Manganese	**26 Fe** Iron
37 Rb Rubidium	**38 Sr** Strontium	**39 Y** Yttrium	**40 Zr** Zirconium	**41 Nb** Niobium	**42 Mo** Molybdenum	**43 Tc** Technetium	**44 Ru** Ruthenium
55 Cs Caesium	**56 Ba** Barium	57–71	**72 Hf** Hafnium	**73 Ta** Tantalum	**74 W** Tungsten	**75 Re** Rhenium	**76 Os** Osmium
87 Fr Francium	**88 Ra** Radium	89–103	**104 Rf** Rutherfordium	**105 Db** Dubnium	**106 Sg** Seaborgium	**107 Bh** Bohrium	**108 Hs** Hassium

57 La Lanthanum	**58 Ce** Cerium	**59 Pr** Praseodymium	**60 Nd** Neodymium	**61 Pm** Promethium	**62 Sm** Samarium
89 Ac Actinium	**90 Th** Thorium	**91 Pa** Protactinium	**92 U** Uranium	**93 Np** Neptunium	**94 Pu** Plutonium

ELEMENT FAMILIES

Blocks of different shades—such as green and orange—are used to group together elements in the same family (see page 12). Elements in a family share similar properties.

KEY

Alkali metals

Alkaline earth metals

Transition metals

Lanthanides

Actinides

Post-transition metals

Metalloids

Nonmetals

Halogens

Noble gases

GROUPS

The table is arranged in 18 columns, known as groups, which run down the table. Elements in the same group have their electrons arranged in a similar way, which gives them similar properties. For example, elements in group 18, such as helium and neon, are mostly clear gases.

18

2
He
Helium

13 14 15 16 17

5 **B** Boron	6 **C** Carbon	7 **N** Nitrogen	8 **O** Oxygen	9 **F** Fluorine	10 **Ne** Neon
13 **Al** Aluminum	14 **Si** Silicon	15 **P** Phosphorus	16 **S** Sulfur	17 **Cl** Chlorine	18 **Ar** Argon

9 10 11 12

27 **Co** Cobalt	28 **Ni** Nickel	29 **Cu** Copper	30 **Zn** Zinc	31 **Ga** Gallium	32 **Ge** Germanium	33 **As** Arsenic	34 **Se** Selenium	35 **Br** Bromine	36 **Kr** Krypton
45 **Rh** Rhodium	46 **Pd** Palladium	47 **Ag** Silver	48 **Cd** Cadmium	49 **In** Indium	50 **Sn** Tin	51 **Sb** Antimony	52 **Te** Tellurium	53 **I** Iodine	54 **Xe** Xenon
77 **Ir** Iridium	78 **Pt** Platinum	79 **Au** Gold	80 **Hg** Mercury	81 **Tl** Thallium	82 **Pb** Lead	83 **Bi** Bismuth	84 **Po** Polonium	85 **At** Astatine	86 **Rn** Radon
109 **Mt** Meitnerium	110 **Ds** Darmstadtium	111 **Rg** Roentgenium	112 **Cn** Copernicium	113 **Nh** Nihonium	114 **Fl** Flerovium	115 **Mc** Moscovium	116 **Lv** Livermorium	117 **Ts** Tennessine	118 **Og** Oganesson

63 **Eu** Europium	64 **Gd** Gadolinium	65 **Tb** Terbium	66 **Dy** Dysprosium	67 **Ho** Holmium	68 **Er** Erbium	69 **Tm** Thulium	70 **Yb** Ytterbium	71 **Lu** Lutetium
95 **Am** Americium	96 **Cm** Curium	97 **Bk** Berkelium	98 **Cf** Californium	99 **Es** Einsteinium	100 **Fm** Fermium	101 **Md** Mendelevium	102 **No** Nobelium	103 **Lr** Lawrencium

Families of Elements

An element family is a group of elements that share properties. Their similar characteristics are due to having the same number of electrons in their outer shell. Elements in the same family are close to each other in the periodic table (see pages 10–11).

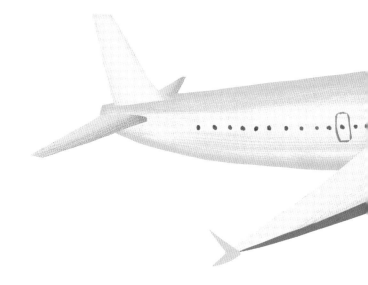

ALKALI METALS

These elements are metals. At room temperature, metals are solid materials that are typically hard, shiny, bendy, and conduct heat and electricity, which means that heat and electricity flow through them. The alkali metals are soft, shiny, lightweight, and very good conductors. They react (see page 22) easily and sometimes violently with other elements.

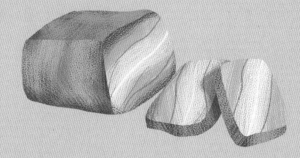

Potassium is so soft that it can be cut with a knife.

ALKALINE EARTH METALS

These metals are harder and heavier than the alkali metals. They are also shiny and very good conductors of heat and electricity. They react with other elements less easily than the alkali metals.

TRANSITION METALS

The largest family, transition metals are harder, stronger, heavier, and melt at a higher temperature than either alkali or alkaline earth metals. They are shiny and very good conductors.

Gold is hard, shiny, and easy to shape, so it is often used for rings and necklaces.

LANTHANIDES

These metals are silvery-white, fairly soft, and do not melt until a high temperature. They react easily with most nonmetals, forming new compounds.

ACTINIDES

These metals are silvery-white, fairly soft, and heavy. They react with most nonmetals. They are all radioactive (see page 28).

POST-TRANSITION METALS

Although these elements share some characteristics with transition metals, they are softer, more breakable, and melt at lower temperatures. They usually conduct less heat and electricity.

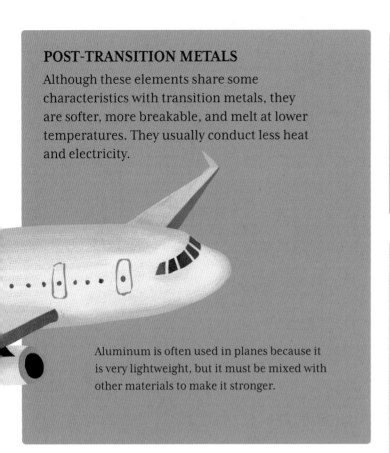

Aluminum is often used in planes because it is very lightweight, but it must be mixed with other materials to make it stronger.

NONMETALS

These elements are not metals, so they are not shiny, bendy, or conductors of heat and electricity. At room temperature, some are gases and some solids.

Along with other living things, humans are made mostly of nonmetals. By mass, your body is 65 percent oxygen, 18.5 percent carbon, 9.5 percent hydrogen, and 3.3 percent nitrogen.

METALLOIDS

Positioned on the periodic table between the metals and nonmetals, these elements usually look like metals, but do not always behave like them. They are shiny, but brittle rather than bendy. They may conduct heat and electricity only under certain conditions.

HALOGENS

At room temperature, some halogens are gases, some liquids, and some solids. Halogens are often toxic, which means they can harm living things. They react easily with other elements, particularly alkali metals.

Chlorine is added to swimming pool water to kill germs.

NOBLE GASES

At room temperature, these elements are clear gases, with no smell or taste. They do not burn easily and do not react easily with other elements.

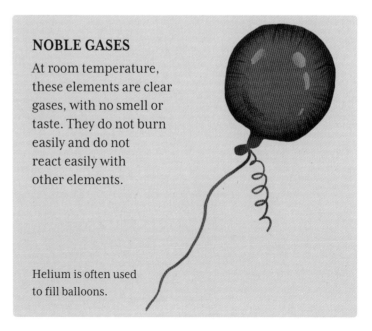

Helium is often used to fill balloons.

Solids

Every element can exist in different states—solid, liquid, and gas—depending on its temperature. These are known as states of matter. If you look around, you will spot many solids, from books to chairs to pencils.

WHAT IS A SOLID?

All solids share some characteristics. A solid can be held. A solid object keeps the same volume at the same temperature, which means it takes up the same amount of space. Most solids have a definite shape. However, some solids—such as a wire or a rubber ball—can be stretched, bent, or flattened.

ATOMS IN A SOLID

In a solid, atoms or molecules are tightly packed and stuck to each other. The atoms cannot easily be pushed aside, which is why you cannot put your hand through a table. Unless atoms are very, very cold—at -273 °C (-459 °F)—atoms are always moving. But the atoms in a solid are tightly joined and lack the movement and energy to change position. However, they do vibrate (shake). This vibration can be seen only with the help of a super-powerful microscope.

The atoms in a solid are stuck together and cannot change their position. This means that a solid does not change its shape to fill a container.

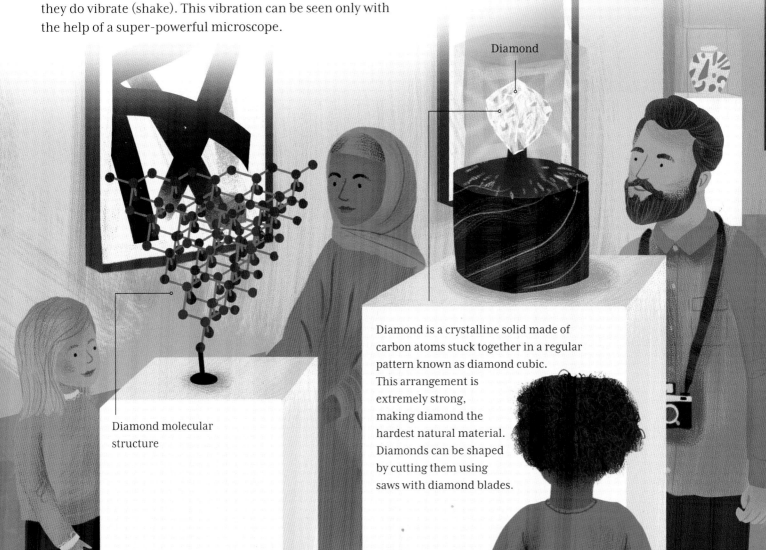

Diamond

Diamond molecular structure

Diamond is a crystalline solid made of carbon atoms stuck together in a regular pattern known as diamond cubic. This arrangement is extremely strong, making diamond the hardest natural material. Diamonds can be shaped by cutting them using saws with diamond blades.

STICKING TOGETHER

Most atoms and molecules are attracted to each other. In a solid, this attraction makes them stick together. This "stickiness" is much weaker than the chemical bonds that join a molecule. However, the vibration of the atoms is too tiny to pull the molecules away from each other.

In most solids, the atoms and molecules are stuck to each other in a regular, repeating pattern. These are known as crystalline solids. In other solids, the atoms or molecules are stuck together more messily and irregularly. These are known as amorphous solids. Glass, wax, and rubber are amorphous solids. They tend to be less hard and strong than crystalline solids.

Scientist Profile

NAME	Ida Noddack
DATES	1896–1978
NATIONALITY	German

BREAKTHROUGH

Along with her husband Walter Noddack and Otto Berg, in 1925 she discovered element 75, rhenium. One of the rarest elements in Earth's crust, it is a heavy transition metal that is solid at any temperature below 3,186 °C (5,767 °F).

Glass is an amorphous solid made of molecules of the compound silicon dioxide (SiO_2), each with one silicon atom joined to two oxygen atoms. The molecules are stuck together irregularly, which makes glass less rigid. While crystalline solids melt at a particular temperature, glass softens and melts gradually over a temperature range, so it can be shaped easily when hot.

Glass

Glass molecular structure

Liquids

When an element gets warm enough, it melts from a solid into a liquid. The most common liquid on Earth is a compound: water. Water covers more than two-thirds of Earth's surface and makes up around 60 percent of the human body.

WHAT IS A LIQUID?

Liquids can be held in a suitable container. They do not have a fixed shape. However, they do have a fixed volume, if their temperature remains the same. This means that, if you pour a carton of milk into different-shaped glasses and bowls, it will take up the same amount of space even though its shape changes.

ATOMS IN A LIQUID

In a liquid, atoms or molecules are quite tightly packed together, but not stuck to each other. This is because the atoms or molecules are warm enough—and vibrating fast enough—to break free from each other. They can move past each other, which allows liquids to flow.

If a liquid is heated, its atoms vibrate faster and move farther apart. This makes liquids expand (get bigger). We make use of this fact in liquid thermometers, in which the liquid in a tube expands, moving up a marked scale, as the temperature rises.

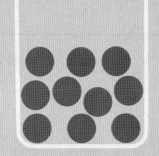

The atoms in a liquid can move past each other, so they flow to cover the bottom of a container.

SLOW FLOW

Some liquids flow faster than others. Some, such as peanut butter, flow so slowly that they can be mistaken for solids. Viscosity is the term that describes how fast a liquid flows. Low-viscosity ("runny") liquids—such as water and juice—have molecules that slide past each other easily.

High-viscosity liquids—such as oil and honey—have molecules that catch on or rub against each other, slowing them down. Usually, larger molecules—such as those in honey—have more difficulty in sliding. However, heating a high-viscosity liquid makes the molecules move farther apart and flow more easily.

Scientist Profile

NAME	Carl Jacob Löwig
DATES	1803–90
NATIONALITY	German

BREAKTHROUGH
He discovered bromine, which (along with mercury) is one of only two elements that are liquid at room temperature. Bromine is not found alone in nature, only in compounds with other elements.

Surface tension is a force that makes the surface of a liquid behave like a skin. Water's high surface tension is caused by water molecules being very attracted to each other. Below the surface, the molecules pull each other in all directions. However, surface molecules have only air above them, so they are pulled only downward, which draws them together to form a skin.

Surface tension allows insects called pond skaters to walk across water. Their long, hairy legs spread their weight across the "skin," so it does not break.

Gases

**Even though you cannot see or smell it, you are surrounded by gas.
The air is a blanket of gases including all-important oxygen, which you
need to breathe. Gas is the third state of matter, but not the last …**

WHAT IS A GAS?

Gases cannot easily be held in your hands. They do not have a fixed shape. They also do not have a fixed volume. This means that, in any container, they always expand to fill all the available space.

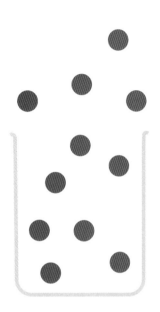

The atoms in a gas fly in all directions, quickly and freely.

ATOMS IN A GAS

In a gas, atoms or molecules are warm enough—giving them enough energy—to dart around freely. If they are packed into a small container, they can be close to each other. If they are not in a container, they can be very far apart.

The atoms and molecules bounce off each other and against the sides of any container. The force of atoms and molecules hitting a container's walls is called "gas pressure."

As a gas gets hotter, its atoms move faster. If a warming gas is in a stretchy container—such as a balloon—the growing pressure of the gas on the inside of the balloon will make the balloon expand.

FOURTH STATE OF MATTER

On Earth, we are familiar with only three states of matter, but a fourth state exists: plasma. To become a plasma, gas has to get extremely hot. On Earth, this usually happens only high in Earth's atmosphere and in lightning. Elsewhere in the Universe, plasma is very common: Stars are made mostly of plasma.

In a plasma, the atoms are so hot that they rip apart, losing electrons. Since electrons have an electric charge (see page 8), this gives plasma an electric charge. When plasma flowing from the Sun meets Earth's atmosphere, the air glows, creating lights called auroras. These can usually be seen only around the poles.

Scientist Profile

NAME   William Ramsay

DATES   1852–1916

NATIONALITY   Scottish

BREAKTHROUGH

In 1898, he and Morris Travers discovered the elements krypton, neon, and xenon, which are found in small quantities in air. He cooled air until it was liquid, then captured the elements as they boiled into gas at different temperatures. These three noble gases are among the 11 elements that are gases at room temperature.

If you let go of a balloon filled with helium gas, it rises into the air. This is partly because helium is lighter than air. Helium has only 2 protons in its atoms, so it is very light. Around 78 percent of air is the heavier gas nitrogen, which has 7 protons in its atoms.

The air beneath the balloon pushes on the balloon with more force than the air above the balloon—so the light balloon moves upward. This is because the pressure of the air beneath the balloon is slightly greater than the pressure of the air above the balloon, because air gets thinner the higher you travel. This is due to the force of gravity (see page 79)—which pulls air toward Earth—getting weaker farther from Earth's surface.

Changes of State

**Elements change from one state to another when they are heated or cooled.
Solids melt into liquids, while liquids freeze into solids.
Liquids evaporate into gases, while gases condense into liquids.**

MELTING AND FREEZING

When a solid element gets warmer, its atoms gain energy. As the atoms vibrate faster, they separate from each other. The solid melts, becoming a liquid. When an element freezes, the reverse happens. As its atoms cool, they have less energy. They slow, move closer, then stick together. These changes are reversible, which means that a melted element can be frozen again—and the other way around.

Melting point is the temperature at which a particular material changes state between solid and liquid. Each element has a different melting point. The element with the lowest melting point is helium, which melts at -272 °C (-458 °F). Carbon has the highest melting point, at 3,550 °C (6,420 °F).

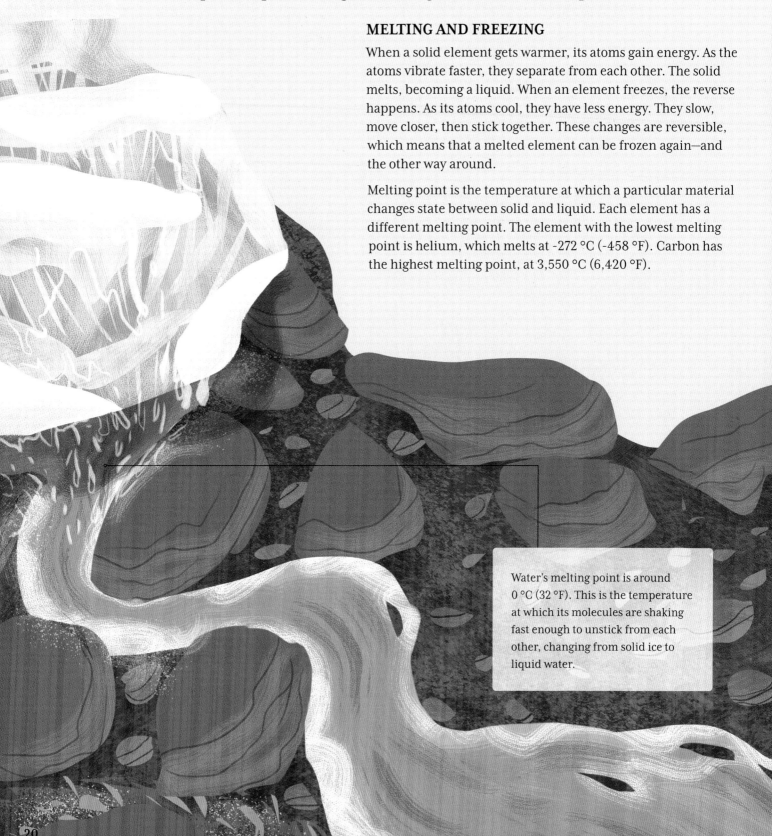

Water's melting point is around 0 °C (32 °F). This is the temperature at which its molecules are shaking fast enough to unstick from each other, changing from solid ice to liquid water.

EVAPORATING AND CONDENSING

Evaporation happens when atoms in a liquid are warm enough—and moving fast enough—to break free from it. The atoms become gas. On a sunny day, evaporation makes puddles dry up within a few hours. However, evaporation happens much faster if a liquid is boiled. This is when its atoms are moving so fast that they form big bubbles of gas that rise to the liquid's surface.

Each element boils at a different temperature, known as its boiling point. Helium has the lowest boiling point, at -269 °C (-452 °F). Tungsten has the highest boiling point: 5,930 °C (10,706 °F).

Condensation happens when a gas is cooled to its boiling point or below. The gas's atoms slow and move closer together, becoming liquid. You can watch condensation happening on the outside of a cold soda glass. As the glass cools the surrounding air, the gaseous water floating in air turns to liquid water on the glass.

Scientist Profile

NAME   Anders Celsius

DATES   1701–44

NATIONALITY   Swedish

BREAKTHROUGH

He developed the Celsius (often written as °C) scale, which we use to measure temperature. His version of the scale measured the boiling point of water as 0 °C and the freezing point as 100 °C, but today those values are reversed.

NO CHANGE

All elements can exist in all states of matter, but not all compounds (see page 9) or mixtures (see page 24) can. That is because many larger molecules break apart when they get too hot, so they do not have a melting or boiling point. Many materials, such as the paper in this book, catch fire if you heat them. However, some common compounds—such as water and glass—do exist in all three states.

Water's boiling point is around 100 °C (212 °F). At this temperature, its molecules break free, forming bubbles of gaseous water, called water vapor, that rise into the air.

Chemical Reactions

A chemical reaction is when two or more materials react to each other, breaking or making chemical bonds between their atoms (see page 9). This makes a new material or materials. Chemical reactions formed all the millions of compounds in the Universe. Here are some examples of reactions.

RUSTING

Although most materials can touch each other without reacting, nearly all metals react to contact with oxygen. Very slowly, the metal iron reacts to the oxygen and water in damp air. The iron's surface takes oxygen atoms, becoming a reddish material called iron oxide, which we often call rust.

COMBUSTION

Also called "burning," combustion is a chemical reaction. Three things are needed for this reaction: heat, a fuel such as wood, and oxygen in the air. The reaction produces ash and the gases carbon dioxide and water vapor. A combustion reaction is useful, because it releases energy from the wood as heat, which can cook food or power machinery. It is also dangerous, since fire can kill.

BIOLUMINESCENCE

Some deep-sea creatures make their own light to attract mates or prey in the dark water. This ability is called bioluminescence. Special body parts create a chemical reaction by combining oxygen with chemicals called luciferase and luciferins. The reaction releases light.

FINGERPRINTING

Police officers use a chemical reaction to see fingerprints at a crime scene. When we touch surfaces, we leave behind invisible fingerprints of sweat and skin oil, in the unique pattern of the ridges on our fingertips. The element iodine reacts to sweat and oil, turning fingerprints brown.

MAKING TOAST

When bread is heated, it undergoes a chemical reaction—and becomes toast. Heat causes a reaction between the bread's sugars and molecules called amino acids. They become brown molecules called melanoidins.
As with many chemical reactions, we know that a reaction has taken place because of a change in the material's appearance. As with most chemical reactions, this change cannot be reversed.

Scientist Profile

NAME   Stephanie Kwolek

DATES   1923–2014

NATIONALITY   Polish-American

BREAKTHROUGH
In 1965, she created the material Kevlar using a reaction between two chemicals: an amine and an acid. This material is so strong that it is used to make bulletproof vests and car brakes.

Mixtures

Many materials are neither made of one pure element nor of one pure compound: They are mixtures. The paper in this book is a mixture! You can also make mixtures in the kitchen by whisking together oil and vinegar or adding raisins to cereal.

A mixture contains two or more elements or compounds. These materials have not reacted together, so their atoms are not chemically bonded. This means that the materials in a mixture keep their own characteristics. They may not be mixed in particular quantities. For example, a mixture of oil and vinegar can contain two spoons of both or two of one and three of the other.

Unlike most chemical reactions, which cannot be reversed, making a mixture is a reversible change: Its materials can be separated again. A mixture of oil and vinegar can be separated by letting the oil, which is lighter, rise to the surface. Air is a mixture that can be separated by cooling it to a liquid, then using a similar method. A mixture of a liquid and solid can be separated with a filter, which has tiny holes that let the liquid pass through.

ROCK

Different types of rocks are mixtures of different ingredients. The common rock granite is a mix of compounds containing elements such as silicon, oxygen, potassium, and aluminum. It may be studded with gemstones such as topaz, which are compounds of fluorine, aluminum, silicon, and oxygen.

SEAWATER

Pure water is a compound of hydrogen and oxygen (see page 9), but seawater is a mixture because it also contains salts and gases, including oxygen. Salts are compounds that can be made by reacting an acid with a base (see page 26). The most common salt in seawater is sodium chloride, which is better known as the "salt" we put on food.

AIR

Held around Earth by our planet's gravity, air is a mixture of gases. It is made up of atoms and molecules of nitrogen (78 percent), oxygen (21 percent), and argon (1 percent), plus smaller amounts of carbon dioxide, neon, helium, methane, krypton, xenon, and water vapor.

WOOD

Wood's main ingredients are big, strong molecules called cellulose and lignin. Both these molecules contain hundreds of carbon, hydrogen, and oxygen atoms, but they are linked to each other in different quantities and patterns. Wood can be made into paper.

STEEL

Steel is commonly used in tools, vehicles, and buildings. It is an alloy: a human-made mixture of elements where at least one is a metal. Alloys give extra useful properties to metals. Steel, a mix of the metal iron and the nonmetal carbon, is stronger than pure iron.

SAND

Sand is mostly fragments of rock and shell, which have been broken by water and wind over many years. The particular ingredients of sand depend on the location of the beach.

Acids and Bases

Apart from water, many of the liquids in your home are acids or bases. Acids include lemon juice and vinegar, while bases include toothpaste and soap. Strong acids and bases are extremely dangerous and must never be touched or eaten.

WHAT IS AN ACID?

Acids have a sour taste. However, strong acids eat away skin and even metal, so must never be tasted. Acids are substances that contain hydrogen atoms and—if added to water—will break apart, releasing hydrogen ions. An ion is an atom or molecule with a positive or negative electric charge because it does not have an equal number of positive protons and negative electrons (see page 8).

A hydrogen ion is a hydrogen atom that has lost its electron, leaving only its proton. This makes it out of balance: It has a positive charge. Strong acids release a lot of hydrogen ions, while weak ones release fewer. The hydrogen ions "try" to find balance by attaching to other substances they meet. This is what makes strong acids dangerous: They create chemical reactions, changing the other substance.

WHAT IS A BASE?

A base is the opposite of an acid. If it can be dissolved in water, it releases hydroxide ions, which are molecules with one hydrogen atom and one oxygen atom, which between them have 10 electrons but only 9 protons. This makes a hydroxide ion out of balance: It has a negative charge. If added to an acid, a base's negative hydroxide ions attract the acid's positive hydrogen ions. This chemical reaction neutralizes the acid, taking away its acidic nature.

Like a strong acid, a strong base is very reactive because it "tries" to find balance by bonding with other materials. A strong base easily breaks down materials such as fats and oils, which is why bases are used in soaps, detergents, and drain cleaners. Strong bases are just as dangerous as strong acids.

The strength of acids and bases is measured on the pH (short for "power, or potential, of hydrogen") scale. The strongest and most dangerous acids have a pH of 0, while the strongest bases have a pH of 14.

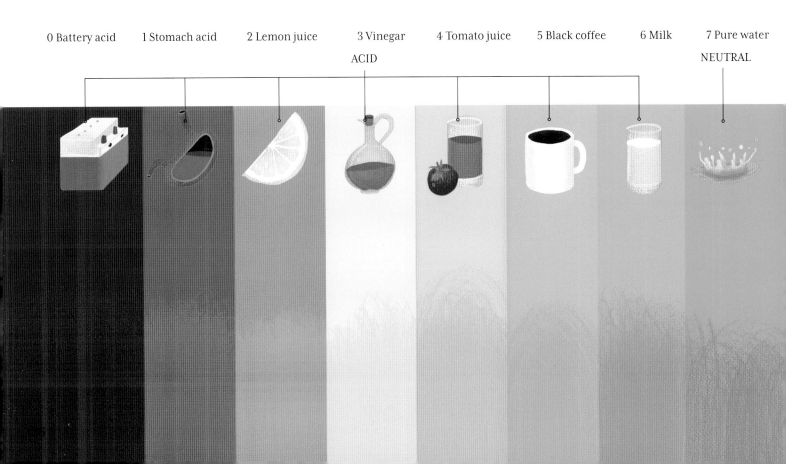

0 Battery acid   1 Stomach acid   2 Lemon juice   3 Vinegar   4 Tomato juice   5 Black coffee   6 Milk   7 Pure water

ACID

NEUTRAL

When the acid hydrogen chloride (HCl) is added to water, it breaks into positive hydrogen ions and negative chloride ions.

When the base sodium hydroxide (NaOH) is added to water, it breaks into negative hydroxide ions and positive sodium ions.

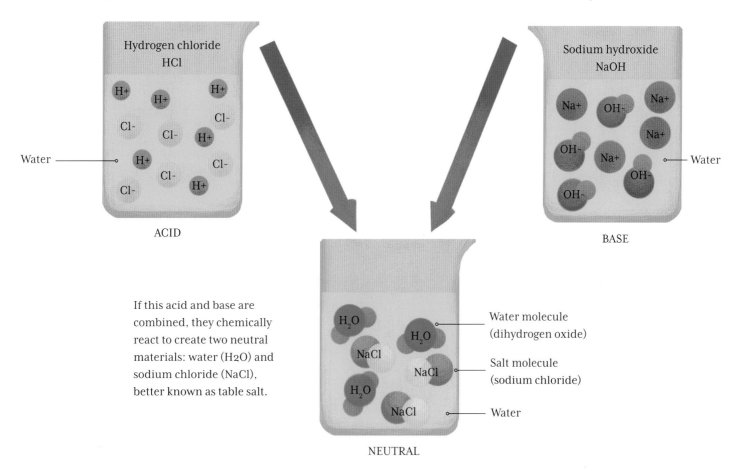

Hydrogen chloride
HCl

H+ H+ H+
Cl- Cl- H+ Cl-
Water H+ Cl-
Cl- H+

ACID

Sodium hydroxide
NaOH

Na+ OH- Na+
Na+
OH- Na+ Water
OH- OH-

BASE

If this acid and base are combined, they chemically react to create two neutral materials: water (H_2O) and sodium chloride (NaCl), better known as table salt.

H_2O
H_2O
NaCl
NaCl
H_2O
NaCl

Water molecule (dihydrogen oxide)

Salt molecule (sodium chloride)

Water

NEUTRAL

8 Toothpaste 9 Baking soda 10 Hand soap 11 Floor cleaner 12 Oven cleaner 13 Toilet bleach 14 Drain cleaner

BASE

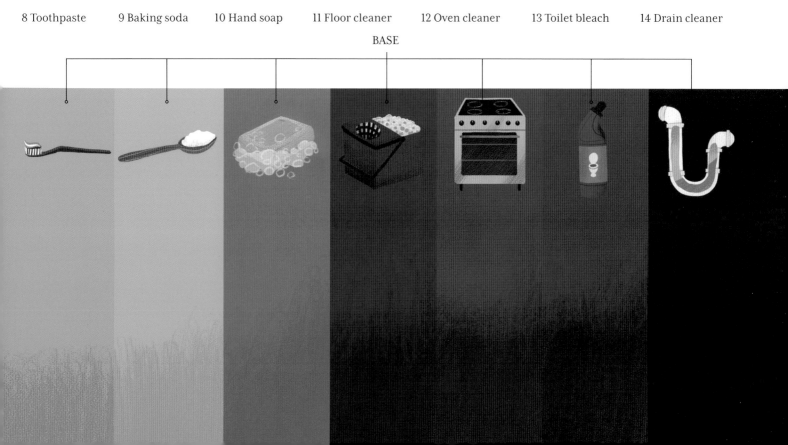

Isotopes

Each element has a particular number of protons, along with—usually—a matching number of electrons. However, every element can exist in different forms, called isotopes, each with a different number of neutrons in its nucleus.

NUMBER OF NEUTRONS

Hydrogen is the element with the fewest isotopes: three. Caesium and xenon have the most known isotopes: 36. Like many elements, hydrogen has one isotope that is most common, while the others are rarer. Nearly all hydrogen atoms in Earth and its atmosphere are the isotope hydrogen-1, with no neutron in their nucleus. The rarer hydrogen-2 isotope has one neutron, while the hydrogen-3 isotope has two neutrons.

Different isotopes of an element have many of the same properties, so the hydrogen isotopes are all gases at room temperature. However, since they have more neutrons, the hydrogen-2 and hydrogen-3 isotopes are heavier. They also have different melting and boiling points.

STABLE AND RADIOACTIVE

There are two types of isotopes: stable and unstable. Stable isotopes do not change over time. Unstable isotopes are also called radioactive isotopes or radioisotopes. These isotopes have too many or too few neutrons to hold the atom together. This is because neutrons and protons exert a pulling force on each other, which holds together the nucleus—but only if they are balanced.

Radioisotopes break apart, which makes them give off energy, known as radiation. A decaying radioisotope atom can—over seconds or over billions of years—lose a neutron, becoming a different isotope; or lose a proton, becoming a different element entirely.

All elements with 83 or more protons (an atomic number of 83 or more), as well as technetium (atomic number 43) and promethium (atomic number 61), have only unstable isotopes. These elements are always radioactive, either weakly or strongly.

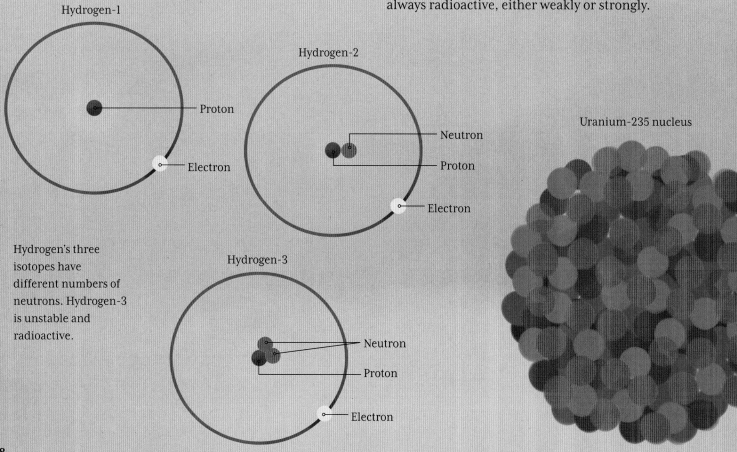

Hydrogen-1

Proton

Electron

Hydrogen-2

Neutron

Proton

Electron

Hydrogen's three isotopes have different numbers of neutrons. Hydrogen-3 is unstable and radioactive.

Hydrogen-3

Neutron

Proton

Electron

Uranium-235 nucleus

USEFUL RADIOISOTOPES

Radiation can be dangerous in large quantities, since it damages living cells. However, when radiation is carefully targeted, it can save lives. For example, the radioactive isotope lead-212 is used to kill cancer cells (see page 74) while limiting damage to healthy cells.

Radioisotopes are also used in power plants to release energy that is harnessed to make electricity. The current method for this is nuclear fission (which means "splitting of the nucleus"). Usually, the nuclei of uranium-235 or plutonium-239 are split. These big, unstable nuclei are easier to split—and release much more energy— than smaller, more stable nuclei.

Scientist Profile

NAME	John Cockcroft and Ernest Walton
DATES	1897–1967 and 1903–95
NATIONALITY	British and Irish

BREAKTHROUGH
In 1932, they were the first to split an atom's nucleus, by firing protons at lithium. This divided each lithium nucleus into two helium nuclei.

Neutron

To start the process of nuclear fission, a nuclear power plant uses a start-up neutron source, such as californium-252. This highly radioactive isotope gives off lots of neutrons.

A neutron shoots at a uranium-235 nucleus, making it split.

Uranium-235 nucleus

Neutron

Two or three neutrons are released, which shoot into more uranium nuclei and split them, repeating the process over and over again. This is known as a chain reaction.

Uranium-235 nucleus

Neutron

Strontium-93 nucleus

Two lighter elements are produced, which are themselves radioactive and must be disposed of carefully.

Xenon-140 nucleus

Energy is released in the form of radiation and heat. The heat is used to boil water to make steam, which turns a generator that converts movement energy into electrical energy.

Energy

Polymers

Polymers are long molecules. They are made of lots of smaller molecules that are chemically bonded to each other in a chain, which can contain as many as millions of atoms. Materials that contain polymers are strong due to these long, often interlinking, chains.

Many polymers are found in nature. All living things contain the polymer DNA (see page 36), the long-lasting molecule that holds the body's complex instructions. In animals, the tough polymer collagen gives strength to muscles and bones. Plants contain the polymers cellulose and lignin (see page 25), which give them shape and stability.

Human-made polymers include plastics. Most plastics are made from fossil fuels (see page 102), but some, known as bioplastics, are made from plants. Plastics are produced by a process called polymerization, which links smaller molecules into a chain. Plastics have been developed with polymers that give properties from rigidity to stretchiness.

HIGH-DENSITY POLYETHYLENE

This plastic is made from fossil fuels, either oil or natural gas. It is strong, long-lasting, and rigid. It is used for playground equipment, as well as pipes and street signs.

WOOL

Sheep's wool is made of molecules called keratins—which are also found in skin, horns, and hooves—linked together into long chains. These polymers make wool strong, bendy, stretchy, and waterproof.

ASPHALT

Also known as bitumen, asphalt is a thick, gooey form of oil, a fossil fuel. Asphalt is often an ingredient in playground and road surfaces, because its polymers make it waterproof, tough, and slightly bouncy—which helps prevent injuries from falls, and cracking from constant use.

POLYSTYRENE

This plastic is often formed into a fluffy foam. Its strength and bendiness allow the foam to absorb the force of blows, so it is used for protection inside helmets, children's car seats, and packaging.

NYLON

Nylon is a human-made polymer that is often used for tights, pantyhose, and other clothing. Made from oil, nylon is formed into thread that can be woven or knitted. It is stretchy and dries quickly after washing.

NATURAL RUBBER

Natural rubber is made from latex, a sticky liquid produced by rubber trees. When latex dries, it is a bouncy solid. A rubber ball bounces because the force of it hitting the ground puts an equal force back onto the ball, making it shoot back up. A ball made of a rigid material would break, but a rubber ball squashes as it hits the ground, then snaps back into shape.

Life

Life began on our planet around 3.8 billion years ago, when tiny, simple living things appeared in the oceans. Over millions of years, these living things changed. Some remained small and simple; some developed stems and leaves; and a few grew brains, beaks, and wings. This slow process, called evolution, has resulted in at least 8 million species on our planet today, from immense whales to microscopic bacteria. A species—such as humans or Scots pine trees—is a group of living things that look similar and breed together to make more of their kind.

Despite their differences, all living things share characteristics. All are made of tiny building blocks called cells, although some are made of just one cell, and others—such as humans—are made of trillions. Unlike a rock or a shoe, all living things are sensitive to changes in their surroundings, such as light and touch. They can all control the conditions inside themselves, from the beating of their heart to the movement of water through their roots and stems. All living things grow and develop, from a tadpole to a frog, a seed to a tree, a tiny bacterium to a larger one. They can also move at some stage in their life, whether that is the slow growth movements of plants or the speedy running of a cheetah.

All living things need food, which they use for energy. However, their methods of getting food are very different: Animals eat other living things, plants make their own food, and fungi—such as mushrooms—soak up food from their surroundings. Finally, all living things can reproduce, although they do it in many ways. While meerkats give birth to small baby meerkats, bacteria divide into two, and fungi release tiny spores, which develop into new fungi.

The earliest animals evolved in the oceans more than 700 million years ago. They were simple, soft-bodied, and—like today's insects and jellyfish—they were invertebrates, which do not have a backbone.

After studying the giant tortoises of the Pacific Ocean's Galápagos Islands, the British scientist Charles Darwin (1809–82) figured out important ideas about how and why animals evolve. He noticed that tortoises living on islands with tall shrubs and cacti had evolved longer necks and arched shells so they could reach food.

33

Cells

All living things are made of cells. Most cells are too small to be seen by the human eye, with the tiniest 0.00002 cm (0.000008 in) across. One of the largest cells, up to 30 cm (12 in) long, belongs to a protist known as a seaweed. There are two types of cells: prokaryotic and eukaryotic.

PROKARYOTIC CELLS

Prokaryotic cells were the first form of life on Earth. Those first prokaryotes were unicellular organisms, which means they were living things made of just one cell. Today's prokaryotes belong to two groups—bacteria and archaea—which are both unicellular and too tiny to be seen without a microscope. Prokaryotic cells are smaller and simpler than eukaryotic cells. Unlike eukaryotic cells, they do not have a central structure called a nucleus, where deoxyribonucleic acid (DNA; see page 36) is stored.

Scientist Profile

NAME   Robert Hooke
DATES   1635–1733
NATIONALITY   English
BREAKTHROUGH
In 1665, he discovered cells when examining plants through a microscope. He named them "cells" from the Latin word *cellula*, meaning "small room."

Inside a typical prokaryotic cell

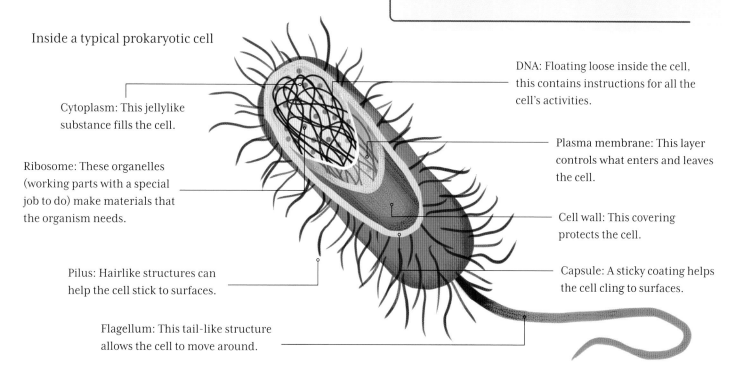

Cytoplasm: This jellylike substance fills the cell.

Ribosome: These organelles (working parts with a special job to do) make materials that the organism needs.

Pilus: Hairlike structures can help the cell stick to surfaces.

Flagellum: This tail-like structure allows the cell to move around.

DNA: Floating loose inside the cell, this contains instructions for all the cell's activities.

Plasma membrane: This layer controls what enters and leaves the cell.

Cell wall: This covering protects the cell.

Capsule: A sticky coating helps the cell cling to surfaces.

PROKARYOTES

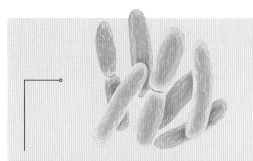

Bacteria: These unicellular microorganisms are found on land, in water, and inside other living things, where some cause disease.

Archaea: Made of different materials from bacteria, these unicellular organisms live nearly everywhere on Earth, including extreme environments such as deep underground.

EUKARYOTIC CELLS

The first eukaryotic cells evolved from prokaryotic cells around 2.5 billion years ago. Four groups of living things are made of eukaryotic cells: animals, plants, fungi, and protists. Some are multicellular, which means they are made of many cells, while others are single-celled. In organisms with many cells, all the cells are not identical in shape and function, since they specialize to make different structures, such as skin or hair. In addition, the cells of animals, plants, fungi, and protists have different characteristics to support their different lives. However, most eukaryotic cells share some basic parts, including a nucleus and organelles with their own particular jobs.

Inside a typical animal cell

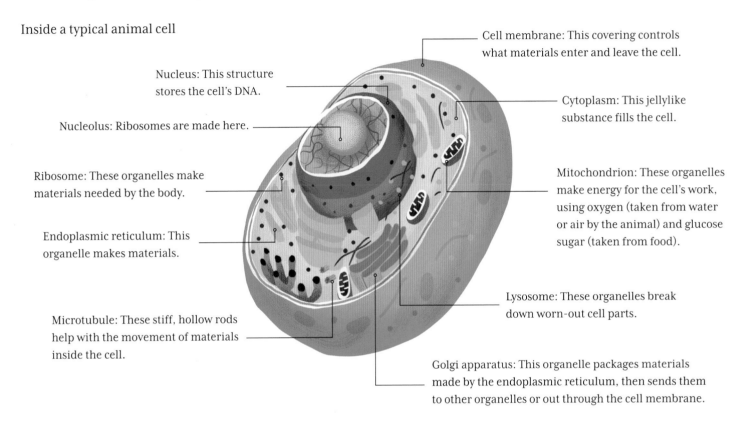

Cell membrane: This covering controls what materials enter and leave the cell.

Nucleus: This structure stores the cell's DNA.

Nucleolus: Ribosomes are made here.

Cytoplasm: This jellylike substance fills the cell.

Ribosome: These organelles make materials needed by the body.

Mitochondrion: These organelles make energy for the cell's work, using oxygen (taken from water or air by the animal) and glucose sugar (taken from food).

Endoplasmic reticulum: This organelle makes materials.

Lysosome: These organelles break down worn-out cell parts.

Microtubule: These stiff, hollow rods help with the movement of materials inside the cell.

Golgi apparatus: This organelle packages materials made by the endoplasmic reticulum, then sends them to other organelles or out through the cell membrane.

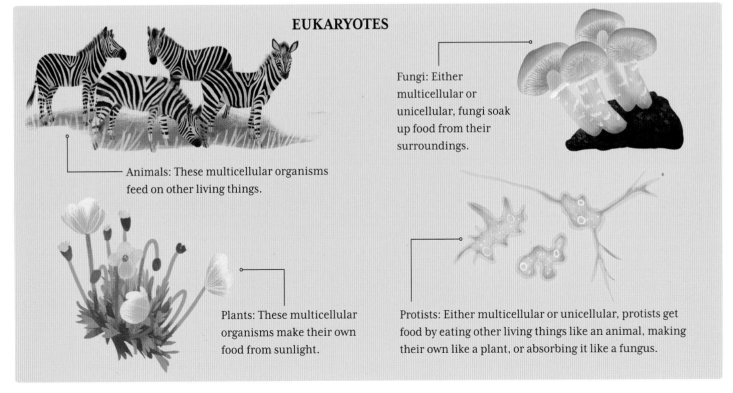

EUKARYOTES

Animals: These multicellular organisms feed on other living things.

Fungi: Either multicellular or unicellular, fungi soak up food from their surroundings.

Plants: These multicellular organisms make their own food from sunlight.

Protists: Either multicellular or unicellular, protists get food by eating other living things like an animal, making their own like a plant, or absorbing it like a fungus.

DNA

Strands of deoxyribonucleic acid (DNA) are in the cells of every living thing. DNA contains the recipe for each organism, with instructions for its appearance and the workings of its body. If the DNA strands in one human cell were stretched out, they would be 2 m (6.6 ft) long.

DOUBLE HELIX

DNA strands are the shape of a twisted ladder, known as a double helix. The rungs of the ladder are made of four chemicals: adenine, thymine, cytosine, and guanine. Each rung contains two chemicals: Adenine always forms rungs by pairing with thymine, and cytosine always pairs with guanine. Each short section of DNA—containing different patterns of rungs—holds a separate instruction, known as a gene.

This is easier to understand if you think of DNA as a language, with the four chemicals as its letters. Different combinations of "letters" spell out different "words," which are an individual gene. Human DNA contains 20,000 to 25,000 genes, each gene giving a particular instruction for which materials your cells make, how your organs work, or how you look.

Cells frequently split in two to make a new cell, so that the organism can grow bigger, repair itself, or reproduce. When a cell divides, a new copy of its DNA is needed. This is achieved easily, because of the way DNA's rungs are constructed. Just before a cell divides, its DNA splits down the middle of the ladder, creating two new strands that are then completed by adding the matching chemical to make each rung: Adenine joins thymine, and cytosine joins guanine.

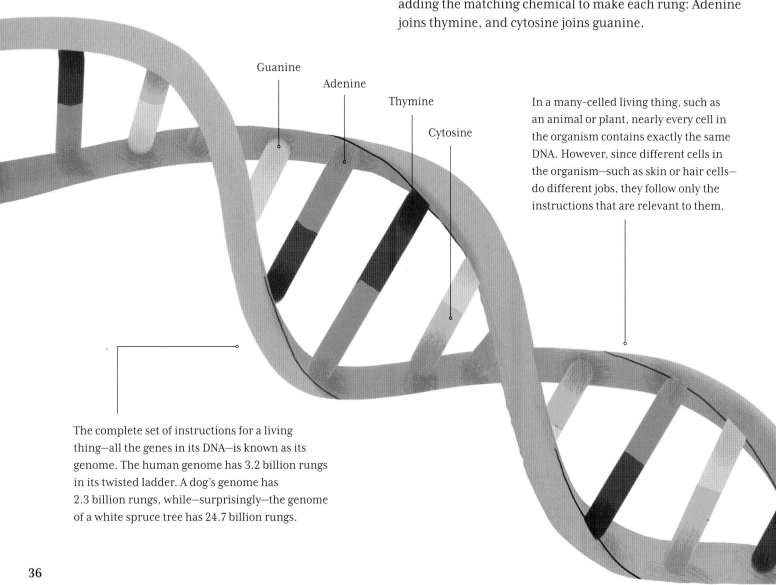

Guanine

Adenine

Thymine

Cytosine

In a many-celled living thing, such as an animal or plant, nearly every cell in the organism contains exactly the same DNA. However, since different cells in the organism—such as skin or hair cells—do different jobs, they follow only the instructions that are relevant to them.

The complete set of instructions for a living thing—all the genes in its DNA—is known as its genome. The human genome has 3.2 billion rungs in its twisted ladder. A dog's genome has 2.3 billion rungs, while—surprisingly—the genome of a white spruce tree has 24.7 billion rungs.

CHROMOSOMES

Most of the time, DNA is loosely coiled inside a cell's nucleus, but before a cell divides, each strand of DNA coils more tightly into a finger-like structure, called a chromosome, to prevent tangling. Different living things have different numbers of chromosomes: Bacteria have just 1 chromosome, while humans have 23 pairs of chromosomes (46 in total).

The 23rd pair of chromosomes determines the sex a baby is born with: Two big "X" chromosomes mean your birth sex is female, while an "X" and a small "Y" chromosome make your birth sex male.

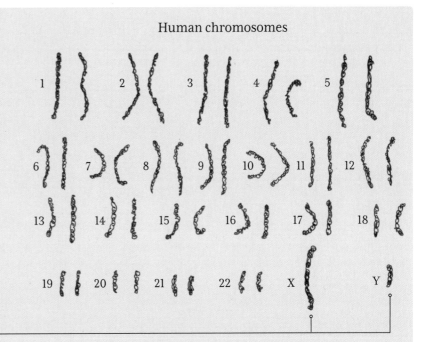

Human chromosomes

INHERITANCE

Most animals—as well as many plants and some fungi and protists—reproduce sexually, which is when a cell from a male joins with a cell from a female in the same species. In these living things, their chromosomes are in pairs, half of each pair from the mother, half from the father. This is how characteristics, such as height and hair color, are passed on in DNA from both parents.

Single-celled organisms usually reproduce asexually, without the help of another organism. For example, many bacteria and archaea simply divide themselves into two. Their offspring are copies of themselves, with just one set of chromosomes.

Scientist Profile

NAME   Gregor Mendel

DATES   1822–84

NATIONALITY   German-Czech

BREAKTHROUGH

By studying pea plants, he figured out rules about inheritance in plants and animals. Some characteristics, such as round peas—or brown eyes in humans—are "dominant," so they are more likely to appear in offspring if either parent has that characteristic. Other characteristics, such as wrinkled peas—or blue eyes in humans—are "recessive," so may not appear in offspring.

Evolution

Evolution is the process through which living things change, generation by generation. This process has allowed living things to adapt to all Earth's habitats, from seafloors to deserts to mountaintops.

Evolution allows living things to adapt to their environment, so that they are suited to finding food and shelter. Over thousands or millions of years, it allowed living things to move into new habitats, where there was less competition for resources. It allowed some to move from the ocean onto land, then later to evolve wings so they could fly or to evolve large paws so they could burrow underground.

Evolution can take place because parents pass on characteristics to their offspring through their DNA. In any species, there are slight differences in characteristics,

so one giant tortoise may have a longer neck than the rest. Sometimes, a difference is so useful—such as a longer neck that allows a tortoise to reach more food—that the tortoise has a better chance of surviving to adulthood than other tortoises. That tortoise passes on its long neck to its babies, which pass on their long necks. Over time, long-necked tortoises become common, while short necks die out. This process is called natural selection.

When a species has been through lots of changes, scientists call it a new species. As habitats change and new competitors evolve, other species become extinct.

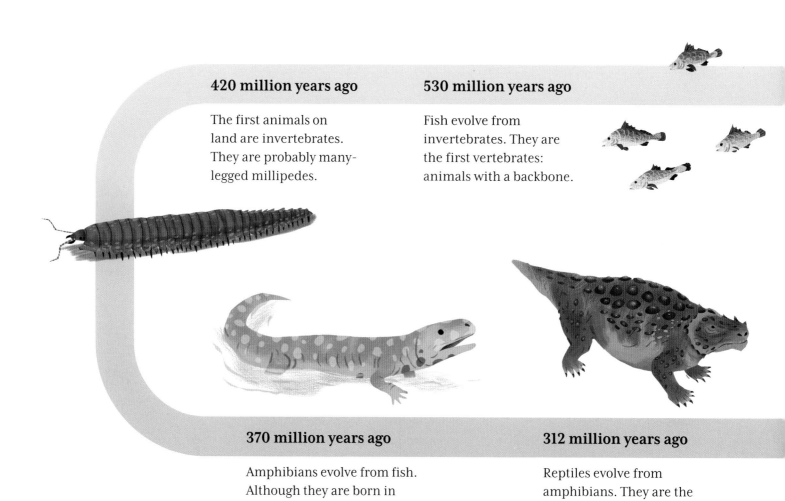

420 million years ago

The first animals on land are invertebrates. They are probably many-legged millipedes.

530 million years ago

Fish evolve from invertebrates. They are the first vertebrates: animals with a backbone.

370 million years ago

Amphibians evolve from fish. Although they are born in water, amphibians are the first vertebrate animals to spend time on land.

312 million years ago

Reptiles evolve from amphibians. They are the first vertebrates to spend their whole lives on land.

4.5 billion years ago

Earth forms in a cloud of dust around the young Sun.

3.8 billion years ago

Prokaryotic cells appear in the oceans.

2.5 billion years ago

Simple eukaryotes evolve from prokaryotes.

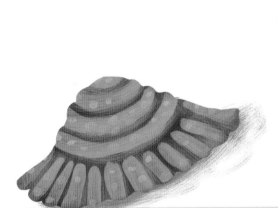

700 million years ago

Animals evolve from ocean-living protists that live in groups called colonies. These first animals are invertebrates: animals without a backbone.

700 million years ago

Plants evolve from ocean-living seaweeds, which are plantlike protists.

1 billion years ago

Fungi evolve in the oceans.

233 million years ago

A group of reptiles called dinosaurs evolves. They walk with their legs directly beneath their body, so they can take bigger, faster strides.

225 million years ago

Mammals evolve, with hair and larger brains than other animals.

72 million years ago

Birds evolve from a group of small, feathered dinosaurs.

Microorganisms

There are many millions of species of microorganisms, many of them yet to be discovered. Microorganisms are living things that can be seen only with a microscope. They belong to all groups of living things, but most are bacteria, archaea, protists, or fungi. Scientists often include viruses among microorganisms, although they are not true living things.

LACTOBACILLUS ACIDOPHILUS

Humans have millions of these bacteria in their intestines, where they get energy by soaking up passing food. Most babies get their first lactobacilli from their mother before they even take their first breath. These bacteria are helpful to humans, as they help us digest food.

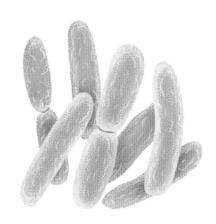

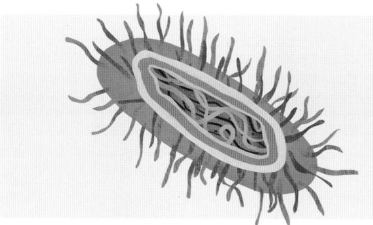

MYCOBACTERIUM TUBERCULOSIS

This bacterium (pictured in cutaway) can infect human lungs, leading to the disease tuberculosis. Spread from person to person by sneezes and coughs, tuberculosis causes coughing, fever, and possibly death. Today, it is prevented by vaccination (see page 75) and treated by antibiotics (medications that kill bacteria).

Scientist Profile

NAME	Elizabeth Bugie
DATES	1920–2001
NATIONALITY	American

BREAKTHROUGH
In 1943, she helped develop the medication streptomycin, the first antibiotic that could kill *Mycobacterium tuberculosis*. Streptomycin is itself made by the bacterium *Streptomyces griseus*, which lives in soil.

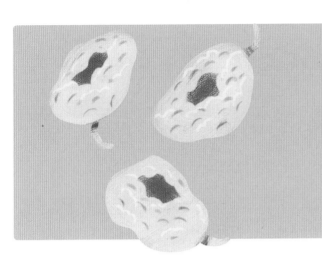

SULFOLOBUS SOLFATARICUS

Like many other archaea, *Sulfolobus* lives in an extreme environment: hot springs where the water is heated by a volcano to 80 °C (176 °F), far too hot for most living things. *Sulfolobus* uses a chemical reaction (see page 24) to turn sulfur in the water into energy for itself.

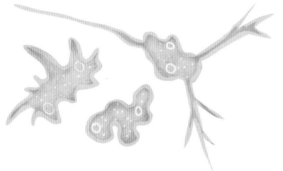

AMOEBA PROTEUS

This protist lives in fresh water. It moves and feeds by changing its shape: It stretches out armlike portions of itself to swim and to trap smaller organisms. These are enclosed by the *Amoeba*, then broken down.

RHINOVIRUS

If this virus gets inside a human's nose or mouth, it can cause a cold. Around 0.000002 cm (0.0000008 in) across, it is spread from person to person by coughs and sneezes. Viruses are not true living things, because they do not grow, move, feed, or respond to the world around them. They are also not made of cells. However, they do contain DNA or a similar molecule called RNA, surrounded by a protective coat. They do reproduce, but only inside a cell belonging to a living thing. Once inside, the virus's RNA instructs the cell to make more viruses. This damages the cell, which can cause disease.

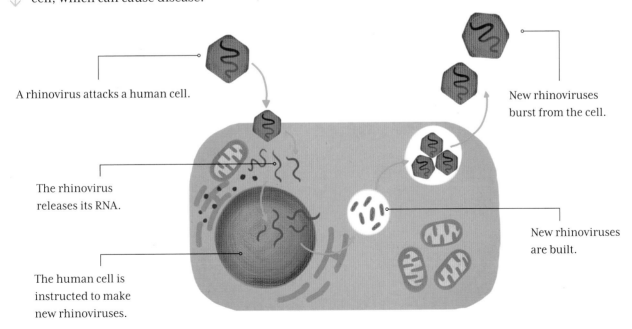

A rhinovirus attacks a human cell.

The rhinovirus releases its RNA.

The human cell is instructed to make new rhinoviruses.

New rhinoviruses burst from the cell.

New rhinoviruses are built.

Plants

There are around 385,000 species of plants, ranging in size from duckweed—only 1 mm (0.04 in) across—to the giant sequoia tree, which grows 95 m (311 ft) tall. Most plants are green and have roots, stems, and leaves. All plants make their own food.

DIFFERENT PLANTS

As long as plants have enough sunlight, warmth, and water, they can grow in habitats from shallow oceans to mountaintops. They have evolved a range of different characteristics to suit different conditions. For example, desert plants, such as cacti, have evolved thick stems where they store water, so they can survive dry periods. Mountain plants grow low to the ground for protection from cold and the drying wind. There are four main groups of plants, all of them found in a wide range of habitats:

Flowering plants: There are more than 350,000 species of flowering small plants, shrubs, and trees (which have a thick, woody stem). Flowering plants have roots, stems, and leaves that are usually broad and flat. They grow flowers that make seeds containing new baby plants.

Coniferous plants: There are around 1,000 species of conifers and their relatives, which are mainly shrubs and trees. They have roots, stems, and leaves shaped like needles or scales. They grow male and female cones. Male cones make pollen, which is carried by the wind or insects to female cones, which then make seeds.

Ferns: There are around 13,000 species of ferns, which range from small to tree-sized. They have roots, stems, and leaves called fronds, which are often divided into feathery leaflets. Instead of making seeds, ferns release tinier, simpler spores, which will develop into new plants.

Rootless plants: There are around 20,000 species of rootless and stemless plants, such as mosses, which are usually small and low-growing. They attach to surfaces and soak up water using hairlike threads called rhizoids. They release spores to make new plants.

MAKING FOOD

Plants make food using a process called photosynthesis. To do this, they need three ingredients: water, carbon dioxide, and sunlight. Most plants take in water from the soil through their roots. Land plants soak up carbon dioxide gas from the air, but water-living plants can take it from water.

Plants soak up sunlight using a green chemical called chlorophyll, which is why most plants look green. Sunlight is energy released by the Sun. Plants use this energy to carry out a chemical reaction (see page 24), which changes water and carbon dioxide into glucose sugar. This sugar travels throughout the plant in tiny tubes, so that every cell can make energy from it.

ESSENTIAL PLANTS

Plants provide shelter and food for other living things. Dead and rotting plants are fed on by bacteria, fungi, and animals such as earthworms. Many other animals—from rabbits to giraffes—feed on living plants. By changing sunlight into glucose, plants create a type of energy that animals can eat. Plant-eating animals pass on some of that energy to the meat-eating animals that feed on them.

In addition, when plants photosynthesize, they release oxygen as a waste product. Before plants—and some bacteria and protists—started to photosynthesize, there was no oxygen in Earth's atmosphere. All animals, and most other living things, need oxygen to survive.

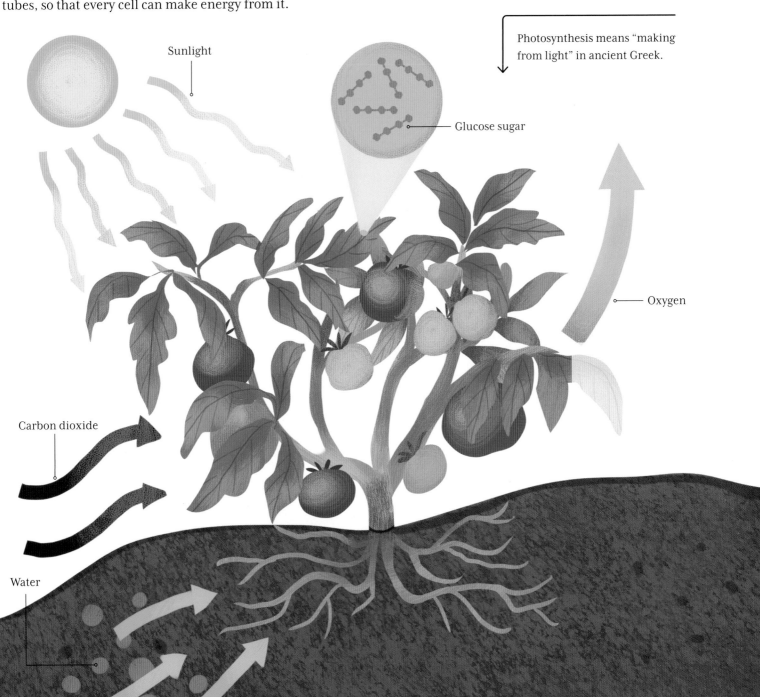

Sunlight

Photosynthesis means "making from light" in ancient Greek.

Glucose sugar

Oxygen

Carbon dioxide

Water

Flowers

Flowers are produced by flowering plants so they can make seeds, which grow into new baby plants. The first step on this journey is pollination, which is when a flower receives a yellow powder called pollen.

FLOWERS

Each flower usually has male and female parts. The male parts, called stamens, make pollen. The female parts include the stigma and ovary, which contains ovules. The stigma is sticky, so it collects pollen easily— usually when it is delivered from the male parts of a different flower. Bits of pollen then travel from the stigma to the ovary. When an ovule receives pollen, it turns into a seed.

POLLINATION

Many flowers are pollinated by animals, including birds, bats, and insects such as bees, wasps, and butterflies. Flowers attract pollinators with their smell or by making a sweet liquid, called nectar. As pollinators visit flower after flower, they carry pollen on their hairy or feathery bodies. Some flowers are pollinated when wind or water carry pollen from another plant.

Stamen

Stigma

Ovary

Ovule

Petal

Sepal

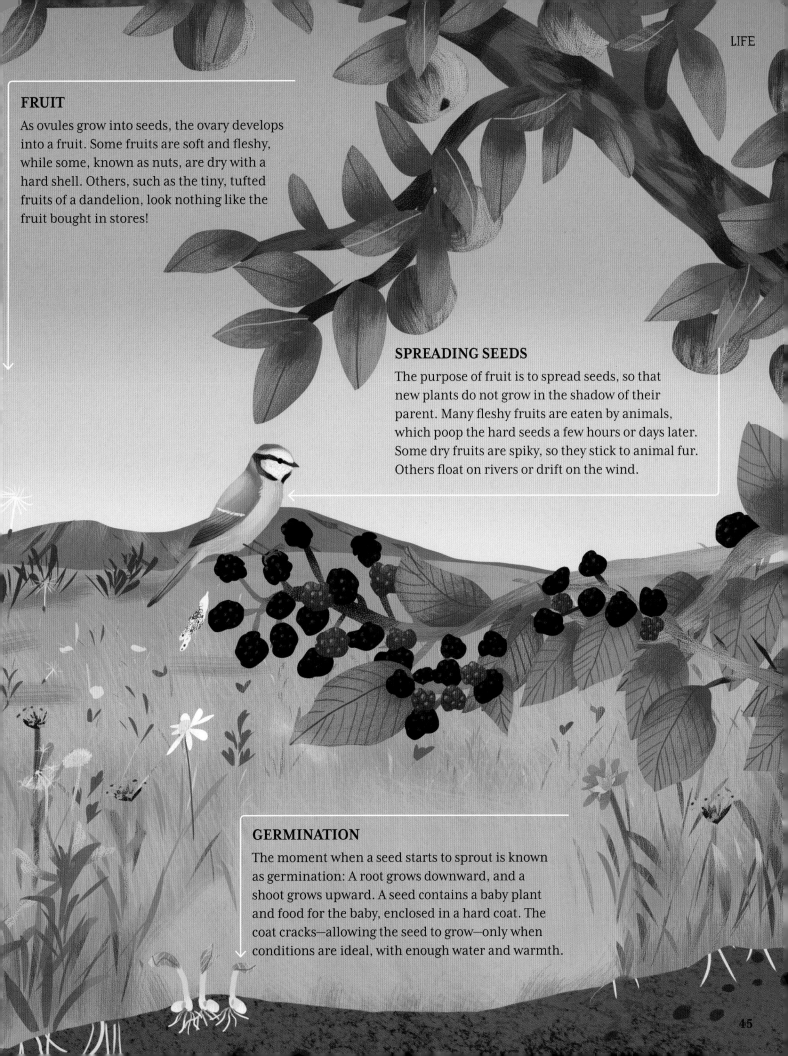

FRUIT

As ovules grow into seeds, the ovary develops into a fruit. Some fruits are soft and fleshy, while some, known as nuts, are dry with a hard shell. Others, such as the tiny, tufted fruits of a dandelion, look nothing like the fruit bought in stores!

SPREADING SEEDS

The purpose of fruit is to spread seeds, so that new plants do not grow in the shadow of their parent. Many fleshy fruits are eaten by animals, which poop the hard seeds a few hours or days later. Some dry fruits are spiky, so they stick to animal fur. Others float on rivers or drift on the wind.

GERMINATION

The moment when a seed starts to sprout is known as germination: A root grows downward, and a shoot grows upward. A seed contains a baby plant and food for the baby, enclosed in a hard coat. The coat cracks—allowing the seed to grow—only when conditions are ideal, with enough water and warmth.

Fungi

Fungi range in size from tiny yeasts to massive, mushroom-sprouting mycelia. Like plants, fungi cannot walk, crawl, or swim from place to place. Unlike plants, they cannot make food: They soak it up from their surroundings. Around 148,000 species of fungi have been named.

Gills

ARMILLARIA OSTOYAE

The biggest living thing may be an *Armillaria ostoyae* in a forest in the United States' Oregon: It spreads over 9.1 sq km (3.5 sq miles). Most of the fungus is underground, where it forms a mass of rootlike threads called a mycelium. Its mushrooms sprout above ground in fall (autumn), when their gills release spores. These are blown away, then grow into new fungi.

BAKER'S YEAST

Around 0.0007 cm (0.0003 in) wide, this single-celled fungus is used by bakers. The yeast soak up sugar in dough, then release the gas carbon dioxide, which makes bread fluffy. These fungi reproduce by budding: A new, identical cell grows from a parent cell.

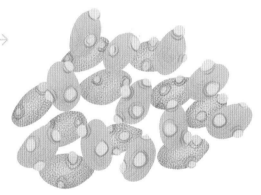

TURKEY TAIL

Named for its mushroom's similarity to a wild turkey's tail, this fungus grows in the logs or stumps of trees. It digests damp wood, making it rot. Wood-rotting fungi are vital in forests, since they return nutrients (materials needed for life and growth) in trees to the soil, where they can be used by new plants.

ZOMBIE-ANT FUNGUS

Found in tropical forests, this fungus lives inside carpenter ants. The fungus soaks up nutrients inside the ant, then sprouts a mushroom. This releases spores that land on more ants and soak their way inside using chemicals.

FLY AGARIC

This fungus soaks up nutrients from rotting plants in woodland soil. It produces mushrooms that are poisonous to humans. The mushrooms can make spores on their own, without contact from another fungus. If the threads of the fungus's mycelium touch another mycelium, it can also reproduce sexually.

PENICILLIUM RUBENS

This fungus often grows as "mold" on fruits and vegetables. Like all fungi, it releases chemicals called enzymes onto the material it is growing on. The enzymes break down the material, which is then absorbed by the fungus.

Scientist Profile

NAME	Alexander Fleming
DATES	1881–1955
NATIONALITY	Scottish

BREAKTHROUGH

In 1928, he discovered that *Penicillium rubens* releases chemicals that kill bacteria which cause infections in humans, including of the eyes, throat, and lungs. This discovery led to the creation of penicillin, the first effective antibiotic medication.

Animals

There are more than 2 million animal species. They belong to six groups: invertebrates, fish, amphibians, reptiles, mammals, and birds. More than 95 percent are invertebrates, which do not have bones inside their body. All the rest are vertebrates, which have a backbone.

Nearly all animals need oxygen (so their cells can make energy), water (to transport materials through their body), and living things to eat (for energy, growth, and repair). Some animals take oxygen from the air using lungs, while others get it from water using gills. These body parts soak up the gas and pass it into the blood. A few animals—including insects—take in oxygen through tiny holes all over their body, while some—including jellyfish—soak it up through their skin.

To get water, some animals drink, some eat living things that contain water, and others soak up water through their skin or gills. Animals also have many diets and ways of finding food. All vertebrates take in food through their mouth, but while some capture smaller animals, others nibble plants or fungi. A few invertebrates do not have a mouth. For example, sponges eat by drawing water into holes in their body, then soak up the tiny living things that are floating in the water.

Periander
metalmark
butterfly

INVERTEBRATES

Invertebrates are found in water, on land, and in the air. Some, such as earthworms, have soft bodies. Others, such as crabs, have a tough covering called an exoskeleton. Some invertebrates have no legs, while millipedes have up to 1,300. Around half of invertebrates are insects, which have an exoskeleton, six legs, a three-part body, and—usually—wings.

FISH

Fish live in water, taking oxygen from it using gills. Most fish have skin protected by small, hard plates known as scales. They have body parts called fins, which help with swimming.

Red-bellied piranha

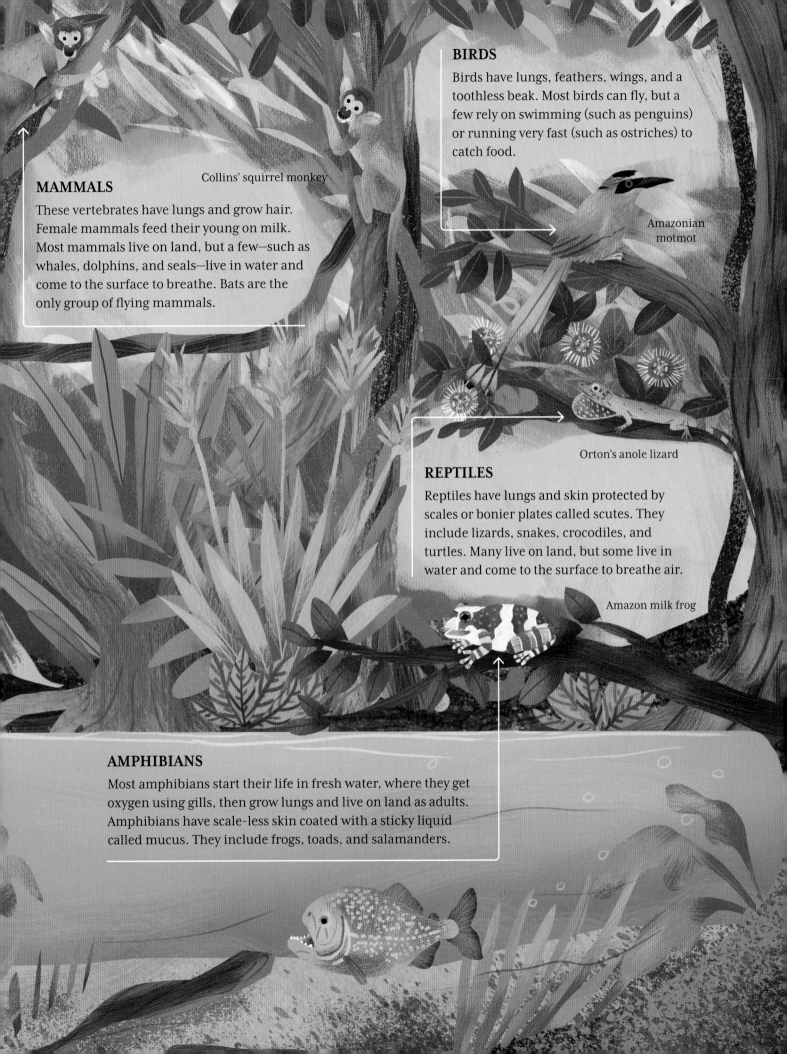

MAMMALS

These vertebrates have lungs and grow hair. Female mammals feed their young on milk. Most mammals live on land, but a few—such as whales, dolphins, and seals—live in water and come to the surface to breathe. Bats are the only group of flying mammals.

Collins' squirrel monkey

BIRDS

Birds have lungs, feathers, wings, and a toothless beak. Most birds can fly, but a few rely on swimming (such as penguins) or running very fast (such as ostriches) to catch food.

Amazonian motmot

Orton's anole lizard

REPTILES

Reptiles have lungs and skin protected by scales or bonier plates called scutes. They include lizards, snakes, crocodiles, and turtles. Many live on land, but some live in water and come to the surface to breathe air.

Amazon milk frog

AMPHIBIANS

Most amphibians start their life in fresh water, where they get oxygen using gills, then grow lungs and live on land as adults. Amphibians have scale-less skin coated with a sticky liquid called mucus. They include frogs, toads, and salamanders.

Life Cycles

Different animal groups have different life cycles, as they are born, develop, and reproduce. Some animals are born looking similar to their parents, but others go through great body changes during their life, known as metamorphosis.

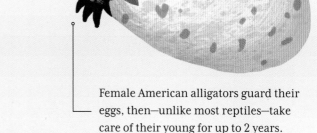

LAYING EGGS

Most animals lay eggs. All birds and most reptiles, amphibians, fish, and invertebrates are egg-layers. Even five species of mammals, called monotremes, lay eggs. Eggs contain a developing baby and, usually, a store of food, known as a yolk. Eggs that are laid out of water—including bird, reptile, mammal, and many insect eggs—have shells, so they do not dry out. Most other animals lay jellylike eggs in water or a damp place.

Female American alligators guard their eggs, then—unlike most reptiles—take care of their young for up to 2 years.

Most fish take no care of their eggs or young, but they usually lay hundreds or thousands of eggs, so there is a good chance that some will survive until adulthood.

GIVING BIRTH

Nearly all mammals give birth to live babies. Larger mammals, such as whales, usually give birth to one baby at a time, but smaller mammals have litters of several babies. Some babies—including human babies—are altricial, which means they are dependent on their parents for care. Others—such as giraffe babies—are precocial, which means they can move and find food soon after birth. A few invertebrates, fish, amphibians, and fish also give birth to live young.

Lion cubs are altricial: Their mother does not teach them how to hunt until they are around 3 months old.

METAMORPHOSIS

Metamorphosis brings about changes in an animal's body, diet, and lifestyle. There are big benefits to metamorphosis: It ensures that young animals eat different food and even live in a different habitat from their parents, so there is no competition between adults and young. Most amphibians, many invertebrates—including insects—and some fish go through metamorphosis.

A fried egg jellyfish is an invertebrate with a complex life cycle.

Each strobila develops into a swimming adult jellyfish, known as a medusa. The medusa traps small living things with its stinging tentacles.

Usually, a female jellyfish releases eggs into water as a male jellyfish releases his sperm, fertilizing the eggs.

Segments, called strobilae, grow and detach from the polyp.

The larva attaches to the seafloor, then grows into a stalk-shaped polyp, with small tentacles that catch tiny living things to eat.

An egg develops into a swimming larva, called a planula.

The striped marsh frog is an amphibian. Most amphibians have a three-stage life cycle: egg, larva, and adult.

Most adults live on land, but stay close to water or live in damp places. They have lungs for breathing air and a wide mouth for eating small animals such as invertebrates.

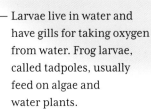

Larvae live in water and have gills for taking oxygen from water. Frog larvae, called tadpoles, usually feed on algae and water plants.

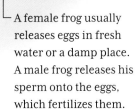

A female frog usually releases eggs in fresh water or a damp place. A male frog releases his sperm onto the eggs, which fertilizes them.

Scientist Profile

NAME   Maria Sybilla Merian
DATES   1647–1717
NATIONALITY   German
BREAKTHROUGH
At a time when most people thought caterpillars and butterflies were different types of animals, she studied the metamorphosis of insects. Her published books contained her own detailed illustrations of how caterpillars metamorphose into butterflies and moths.

Food Chains

Grass, zebras, and lions are linked in a food chain. A food chain is a series of living things that eat each other. At the start of a food chain is a living thing that makes its own food. At the end is an apex predator: an animal that—when it is alive and well—is not eaten by other animals.

PASSING ON ENERGY

A food chain passes energy from one living thing to the next. First in the chain is a living thing called a producer, which makes its own food. Some producers—such as plants, protists such as algae, and some bacteria—make their food from sunlight using photosynthesis. Others, such as many bacteria and archaea, make food from chemicals.

The next link in a food chain is often a small animal, which eats the producer. These animals are called primary consumers. The next link is a larger animal, known as a secondary consumer, which eats the smaller animal.

There are not usually more than around five links in a food chain, since energy is lost at each step. This is because 90 percent of the energy an animal gets from food is used by its own body processes—leaving only 10 percent to be passed up the chain.

This is why there are far fewer apex predators than primary consumers, because large animals—such as lions, great white sharks, and snake eagles—need to eat a lot of smaller animals to get enough energy to survive.

This food chain is one of many in the grasslands of central Africa.

Producer:
White raisin bush

Primary consumer:
Leaf beetle

Secondary consumer:
African pygmy mouse

EXTRA LINKS

A food chain is a simple step-by-step from one animal to the next. Yet in all habitats, different food chains connect with each other, forming complex food webs. For example, lions also eat warthogs, which eat plants, insects, and fungi.

In a healthy habitat, there is usually balance in its food webs, since primary consumers prevent plants from overgrowing—and secondary consumers stop primary consumers from eating all the plants at once. Yet if any living thing disappears, the whole food web may be threatened.

An extra link in most food chains is a final one: detritivores and decomposers. Detritivores are species that eat dead and rotting animals and plants. Detritivores include earthworms and slugs. Decomposers are living things that cannot eat dead things directly, but first break them down using chemicals. Decomposers include fungi and bacteria.

Scientist Profile

NAME	Al-Jahiz
DATES	776–868/9
NATIONALITY	Abbasid (from the region of modern Iraq)

BREAKTHROUGH

In his *Book of the Animals*, he gave the first detailed written descriptions of food chains. He wrote: "Every weak animal eats those weaker than itself. Strong animals cannot escape being eaten by other animals stronger than they."

Quaternary consumer: Brown snake eagle

Tertiary consumer: Black-necked spitting cobra

Habitats

A habitat is the natural home of a living thing, where it is suited to the conditions, such as the level of heat, light, and water. Each habitat—from the rain forest to the desert—is home to different groups of plants, animals, fungi, protists, and microorganisms.

Stretching across the world are large land habitats, called biomes. From rain forest to polar ice, each biome has different conditions due to its climate. Climate is the usual weather in a region. Regions closer to the poles usually have colder, drier climates than those near the equator, where the Sun is more directly overhead. Different plants grow in different biomes, but in very cold or dry biomes, few or no plants grow. In warmer, wetter biomes, there are many plants, providing shelter and food for many other living things.

There are also different water biomes, divided into fresh water and salt water. These are divided yet more: Within the oceans, different communities of living things are found along coasts from on the cold, dark seafloor. Sunlit surface waters are home to many plants and other photosynthesizing life forms, which makes them the most biodiverse water biomes. Biodiversity ("variety of life") is a measure of the number of different species in an area.

POLAR ICE

In the far north and south of our planet, this biome is so cold and dry that no plants can grow. Few animals live here. Larger predatory birds and mammals—kept warm by thick layers of fur, feathers, or fat—hunt prey such as fish in the ocean.

TUNDRA

Found mainly in the far north, in a ring around the polar ice, tundra is a cold, dry biome where only small, tough plants can grow. Animals here have thick fur or feathers, while many fly or walk to warmer regions in winter.

CONIFEROUS FOREST

This biome is mainly in the north, bordering the southern edge of the tundra. Winters are long and cold, but the short summers give trees time to grow. Most trees are conifers, with small, tough, needle-like leaves that are not damaged by cold.

DESERT

This biome has very little rainfall, sometimes because it is far from the rain-bringing ocean. Some deserts are always hot, while others are hot on summer days and freezing during winter nights. The few animals that live here have evolved to survive with little water and to burrow or shelter from extreme heat or cold.

RAIN FOREST

Most rain forests are around the equator, in regions that are always hot and rainy. Trees and other plants grow thickly, most of them with broad, flat leaves that are kept year-round. Rain forests are the most biodiverse of all the biomes.

GRASSLAND

Grassland is found in warm or hot regions with little rain, where only small plants such as grasses can survive. The biome is often home to herds of grass-eating mammals, such as zebras, as well as the animals that prey on them.

TEMPERATE FOREST

With plenty of rain and mild weather, many trees grow in this biome, which is halfway between the poles and equator. In colder parts of the biome, most trees are deciduous, which means they drop their wide, delicate leaves before winter.

Threatened Animals

More than half of animal species are at risk of extinction because of human activities. Governments, conservationists, and many ordinary people are trying to keep them safe by creating new laws, protecting them in national parks, and putting a stop to pollution.

GLOBAL WARMING

As Earth's temperature rises (see page 112), habitats are changing. The ice that covers the ocean around the North Pole is shrinking. This is making it more difficult for polar bears to hunt for seals on the ice, leaving some hungry.

HABITAT LOSS

Wild habitats are lost as farms, cities, and road networks expand. The Javan rhinoceros is one of the world's most endangered animals, with fewer than 100 surviving. It is now found in only one national park in Java, Indonesia, where an area of muddy rain forest is protected.

FISHING AND HUNTING

If too many animals in a species are caught by humans, the remaining animals cannot reproduce fast enough to keep up their numbers. The number of great hammerhead sharks has dropped quickly because it is fished for its fins, which are used in shark-fin soup in parts of Asia.

PET TRADE

Some beautiful animals, such as the Indian star tortoise, are endangered because too many have been caught then sold as pets. Laws now try to protect these animals, ensuring that endangered animals sold as pets must be born in captivity, not captured from the wild.

INVASIVE SPECIES

Invasive species are animals that are not found naturally in a habitat but are introduced there, accidentally or on purpose, by humans. The eastern quoll once lived across much of Australia but is today found on only one island, because it was killed by red foxes brought by English settlers who wanted to enjoy the sport of fox hunting.

POLLUTION

The axolotl is an amphibian that lives only in lakes and ditches around Mexico City, in Mexico. Fewer than 1,000 wild axolotls remain due to the water being polluted by human waste and chemicals from farms and factories.

Scientist Profile

NAME	Paula Kahumbu
BIRTH	1966
NATIONALITY	Kenyan

BREAKTHROUGH

She is helping to protect Kenyan elephants from being hunted for their tusks, which are made of ivory, a hard white material that is illegally carved into trinkets. She campaigns for new laws and works with local people to help elephants.

The Human Body

An average-sized adult is made of around 30 trillion cells—that is a 3 followed by 13 zeros. Cells are the human body's smallest working parts, most of them too tiny to be seen without a microscope. Your body contains around 200 different types of cells, each with a different shape and its own particular work. For example, long brain cells called neurons pass on messages. Blob-shaped stomach cells called chief cells make chemicals that break down food.

Cells group together with similar cells to make tissues, something like the way bricks build a wall. For example, muscle cells form muscles, and skin cells form skin. Different types of tissues join together to form organs. Organs are body parts with a particular job to do. The stomach is an organ with the job of mushing the food you eat, while the heart has the job of pumping blood around your body. You have around 78 organs, ranging in size from your brain's tiny pineal gland—weighing around 0.1 g (0.004 oz)—to your skin, which weighs up to 3.6 kg (8 lb).

Your cells contain even smaller parts including mitochondria. These tiny factories make energy so the cell can do its work. Mitochondria use two main ingredients to make energy: glucose sugar from the food you eat, and oxygen from the air you breathe. Organs including your lungs, heart, and stomach are always busy making sure all your cells have a constant supply of these ingredients. Your body's most important organ, the brain, watches over the work of these organs—and over every other organ in your body.

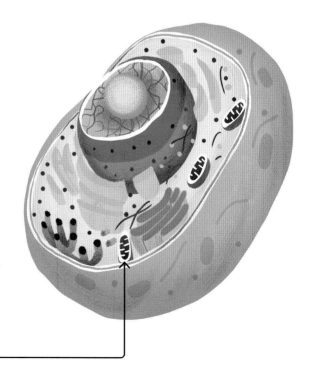

Mitochondria make energy to power a cell's work. Different cells carry out different work, such as making or transporting materials, and—in the case of muscle cells—shortening, so that you can move!

Medicine is the study of the human body, diseases, and how to treat them. In 1864, Rebecca Lee Crumpler was the first African American woman to become a doctor of medicine. She is using an early stethoscope, which helps a person hear sounds inside the body, such as the heartbeat and breathing.

Organ Systems

Your 78 organs are in 11 organ systems. An organ system is a group of organs that work together to do complicated tasks. Your organ systems work with each other to keep your body healthy.

RESPIRATORY SYSTEM

This system carries out the work of breathing: Taking in oxygen so it can be used by cells, then getting rid of a waste gas called carbon dioxide (see page 68).

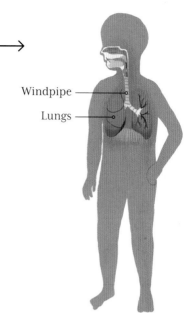

Windpipe

Lungs

DIGESTIVE SYSTEM

The digestive system breaks down food into smaller, useful parts—called nutrients— that can be used by cells (see page 70).

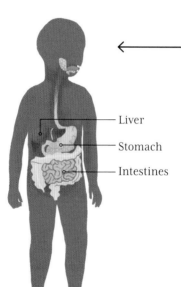

Liver

Stomach

Intestines

CIRCULATORY SYSTEM

This system's heaviest organ is the heart, which pumps blood around the body through tubes called blood vessels (see page 69). Blood carries oxygen, nutrients, and hormones to where they are needed, as well as carrying away waste made by cells and organs.

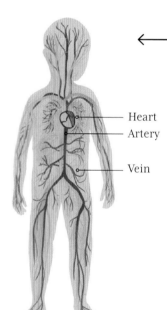

Heart

Artery

Vein

URINARY SYSTEM

The urinary system gets rid of waste made by cells and organs. The kidneys filter waste and water out of the blood, creating a liquid called urine (pee). Urine is stored in a bag-like organ called the bladder until you use the toilet.

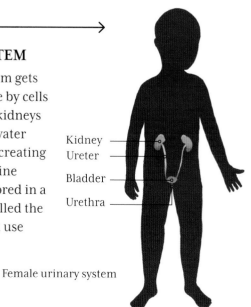

Kidney

Ureter

Bladder

Urethra

Female urinary system

ENDOCRINE SYSTEM

This system is made up of organs, called glands, that make hormones. These chemicals carry messages through the blood, instructing particular organs to change their activities. For example, growth hormone, made in the pituitary gland, tells your bones and muscles to grow during childhood.

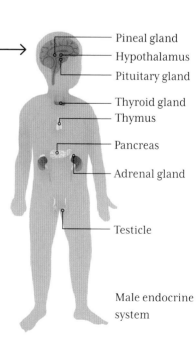

Pineal gland

Hypothalamus

Pituitary gland

Thyroid gland

Thymus

Pancreas

Adrenal gland

Testicle

Male endocrine system

LYMPHATIC SYSTEM

The lymphatic system makes and releases lymphocytes (a type of white blood cell), which target and kill invaders such as viruses and bacteria. The system also collects excess liquid from your tissues and returns it to the blood to keep your fluid levels healthy.

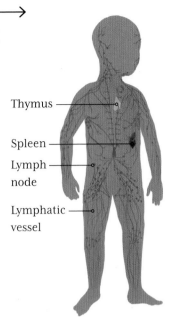

Thymus

Spleen

Lymph node

Lymphatic vessel

INTEGUMENTARY SYSTEM

Your skin, hair, and nails form this system, which helps protect you from infection and from getting too hot, cold, wet, or dry. The skin's sweat glands cool you down as sweat uses your body heat to evaporate (see page 21).

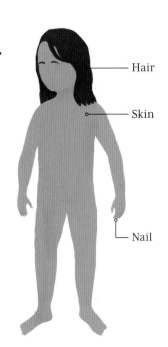

Hair

Skin

Nail

SKELETAL SYSTEM

The skeletal system is made up of your bones, which form a strong frame that gives your body shape, protects your organs, and helps you move (see page 62).

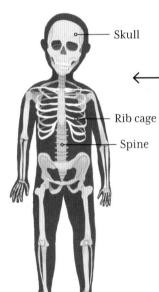

Skull

Rib cage

Spine

MUSCULAR SYSTEM

You have three types of muscle: Skeletal muscle allows your bones to move (see page 63); heart muscle makes your heart beat; and smooth muscle is found in the walls of organs.

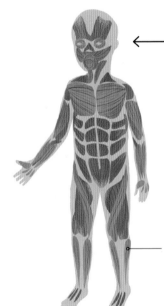

Skeletal muscle

REPRODUCTIVE SYSTEM

This system allows adults to make babies (see page 72). Female reproductive organs include the ovaries and uterus, while male organs include the testicles and penis.

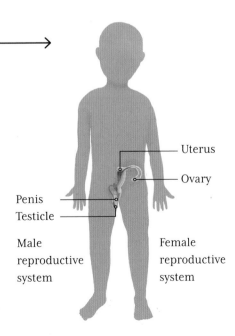

Uterus

Ovary

Penis

Testicle

Male reproductive system

Female reproductive system

NERVOUS SYSTEM

The nervous system is made up of the brain, sense organs including the eyes and ears, and nerves, along which messages travel between the brain and body. This system controls the body's activities, lets you respond to the world, and allows you to think and learn.

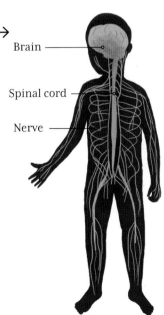

Brain

Spinal cord

Nerve

Bones and Muscles

Most adults have around 206 bones and over 650 skeletal muscles. The longest bone is the femur (thigh bone), and the longest muscle is the thigh's sartorius, both of them over 50 cm (20 in) long in tall adults. Your bones and muscles work together so you can run and jump.

BONE TYPES

Bones with different jobs have different sizes and shapes. In your arms and legs are long bones that give the body strength and balance. Small, cube-shaped bones in your wrists and ankles allow a wide range of movements. Flat, plate-like bones in the skull and ribcage protect your organs.

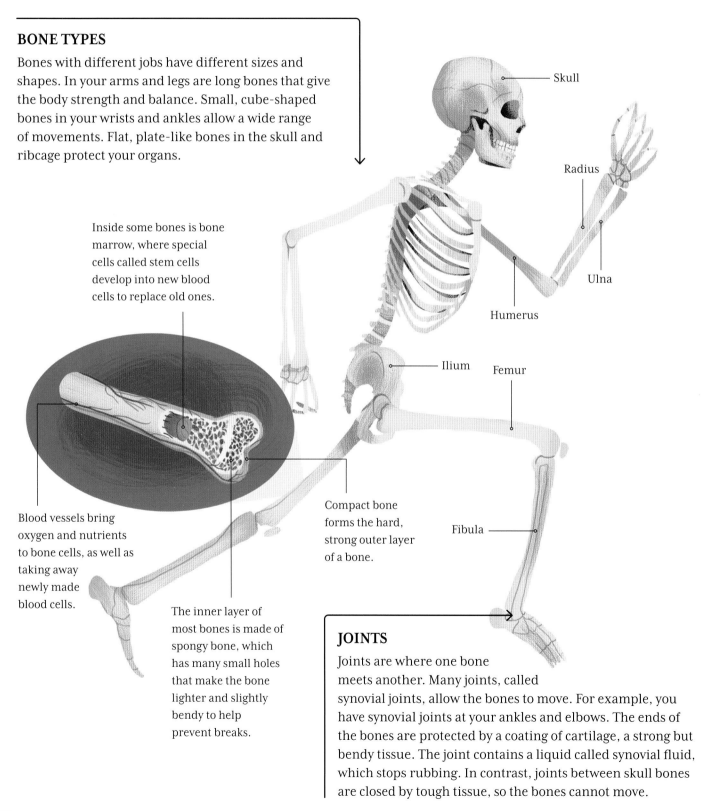

Inside some bones is bone marrow, where special cells called stem cells develop into new blood cells to replace old ones.

Blood vessels bring oxygen and nutrients to bone cells, as well as taking away newly made blood cells.

The inner layer of most bones is made of spongy bone, which has many small holes that make the bone lighter and slightly bendy to help prevent breaks.

Compact bone forms the hard, strong outer layer of a bone.

Skull

Radius

Ulna

Humerus

Ilium

Femur

Fibula

JOINTS

Joints are where one bone meets another. Many joints, called synovial joints, allow the bones to move. For example, you have synovial joints at your ankles and elbows. The ends of the bones are protected by a coating of cartilage, a strong but bendy tissue. The joint contains a liquid called synovial fluid, which stops rubbing. In contrast, joints between skull bones are closed by tough tissue, so the bones cannot move.

MUSCLE MOVES

Skeletal muscles pull on your bones so you can move. A muscle gets the instruction to pull from the brain: The command travels in the form of an electrical signal, from the brain, down the spinal cord, and along nerves to the muscle. Muscles can only contract, making them shorter, which means they can only pull bones, not push them. For this reason, muscles usually work in pairs, with one pulling a bone one direction and the other pulling it the opposite way.

Scientist Profile

NAME   Luigi Galvani

DATES   1737–98

NATIONALITY   Italian

BREAKTHROUGH

In 1780, he discovered that the legs of a dead frog would twitch when touched with an electric spark. This began the study of bioelectricity, which is the electricity made by animal cells to send messages, such as from the brain of a frog to its leg muscles.

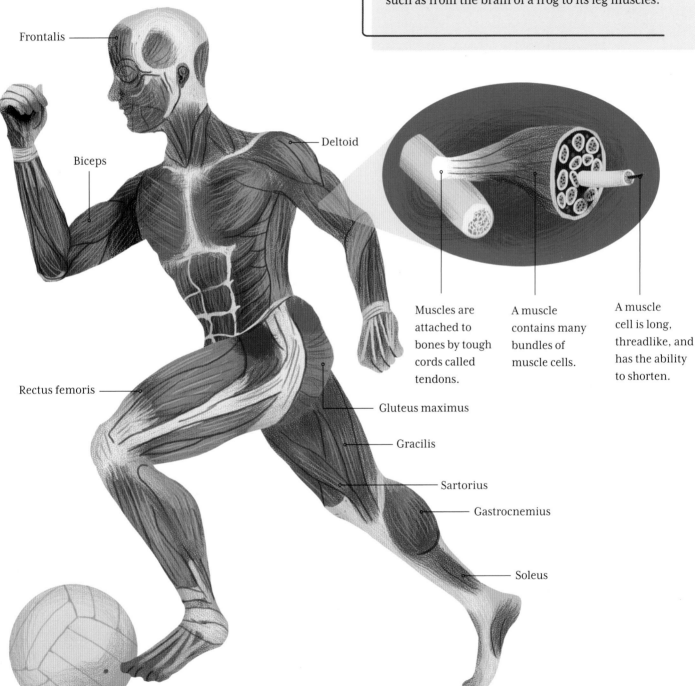

Frontalis

Biceps

Deltoid

Muscles are attached to bones by tough cords called tendons.

A muscle contains many bundles of muscle cells.

A muscle cell is long, threadlike, and has the ability to shorten.

Rectus femoris

Gluteus maximus

Gracilis

Sartorius

Gastrocnemius

Soleus

The Brain

An adult's brain weighs around 1.3 kg (2.9 lb), about as much as a pineapple. The brain has two main areas of work: conscious thoughts and unconscious activities, which you are unaware of—but keep you healthy.

Your brain has three main parts: cerebrum, cerebellum, and brainstem. The surface layer of the cerebrum is where most of your conscious thoughts— your decision to read a book or wave to a friend—take place. These thoughts are created by billions of tiny brain cells, called neurons, sending electrical signals to each other. The cerebellum and brainstem are in charge of most unconscious activities.

The cerebrum is in left and right halves, called hemispheres, connected to each other by nerves. The left and right hemispheres are almost mirror images of each other. The left hemisphere controls the right side of your body, while the right hemisphere controls the left side. Both sides work together on most tasks. Each hemisphere is divided into four regions, called lobes, by deep wrinkles. Each of the four lobes focuses on particular areas of work.

FRONTAL LOBE

The frontal lobe of the cerebrum is focused on planning, making decisions, and solving problems. It also helps you control how you talk and behave with other people.

TEMPORAL LOBE

The cerebrum's temporal lobe processes information from the nose and ears. It helps you to understand what people say and to enjoy music.

PARIETAL LOBE

The cerebrum's parietal lobe helps you understand what you touch and taste. It also helps you know where your body is in relation to other people and objects.

OCCIPITAL LOBE

This lobe of the cerebrum helps you understand signals from your eyes. It allows you to identify objects that you see and to recognize people's faces.

CEREBELLUM

Without you noticing, the cerebellum co-ordinates your movements so, for example, you can walk without falling over. The cerebrum sends muscles the commands to move, but the cerebellum adjusts the commands as it gets information from the body about the position of your legs and arms.

BRAINSTEM

The brainstem keeps your heart beating and your lungs breathing, speeding them up if your muscles need more energy when you are running. It also makes you aware of your surroundings when you are awake, then helps you lose awareness as you drift off to sleep.

Senses

You have five main senses, which give your brain information about the world around you. Your sense organs include your eyes for sight, ears for hearing, nose for smell, mouth and nose for taste, and skin for touch.

SIGHT

Sunlight (or light from a lamp) bounces off objects and into your eyes. First, light travels through the eye's see-through coating: the cornea. Then it enters a hole, called the pupil, and travels through a lens. The curved shapes of the cornea and lens bend the light to make a focused image of the object on the retina, at the back of the eye. The retina has 95 million light-sensitive cells: Each one turns its section of the image into an electrical signal, which travels along a nerve to the brain.

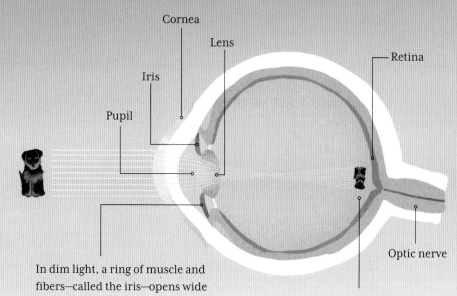

Cornea

Lens

Iris

Pupil

Retina

Optic nerve

In dim light, a ring of muscle and fibers—called the iris—opens wide to let more light into the pupil. In bright light, the iris closes partly so the eye is not dazzled.

The cornea and lens bend light so the image on the retina is upside down, but the brain corrects it.

TOUCH

Your skin contains different types of sensitive cells, which respond to touch, pain, heat, or cold. The cells send electrical signals along nerves to the brain. If you prick your finger, the signal travels along your arm at up to 2 m (6.6 ft) per second.

HEARING

Sounds are made by vibrations: shaking often too small to see. When you bang a drum, its skin vibrates. When you speak, breathed-out air shakes bands of tissue—called vocal cords—in your throat's voice box (see page 68).

The vibration makes surrounding air molecules vibrate. Then these molecules pass on their shaking to surrounding molecules, creating a "sound wave" that travels through the air in all directions.

Eardrum

Hammer

Anvil

Stirrup

Cochlea

Auditory nerve

3. The vibration reaches a liquid-filled organ called the cochlea. The liquid swirls, moving tiny hairlike cells, which pass on signals to your brain along the auditory nerve.

2. The eardrum shakes three small bones, called the hammer, anvil, and stirrup.

1. When a sound wave reaches your ears, it shakes a flap of tissue, called the eardrum.

SMELL

Things like flowers and food release smell molecules that float into your nose. At the back of your nose are sensitive cells that respond to smells, then send signals to your brain. Your brain can detect up to 1 trillion different smells.

TASTE

Your tongue, mouth, and throat are dotted with cells that detect five tastes: sweetness, sourness, saltiness, bitterness, and savoriness. Each food is a mixture of these tastes. As you chew food, some molecules float into your nose through the throat, allowing your smell cells to help your taste cells, giving you a fuller sense of your food.

Lungs and Heart

Your lungs are the largest organ in the respiratory system, while your heart is the chief organ of the circulatory system. The lungs are in charge of breathing in oxygen, while the heart makes sure oxygen is delivered to every cell in your body.

BREATHING

When you breathe in, you take in fuel for your cells: oxygen. When you breathe out, you get rid of a waste gas made by cells as they turn oxygen and glucose into energy: carbon dioxide. You also breathe out unwanted gases found in the air, including nitrogen.

When you breathe in, you pull down a muscle called the diaphragm. This makes more space for your lungs, so air rushes in through your nose or mouth to fill the emptiness. Then, when you breathe out, you relax your diaphragm so it presses on your lungs, making used air rush out.

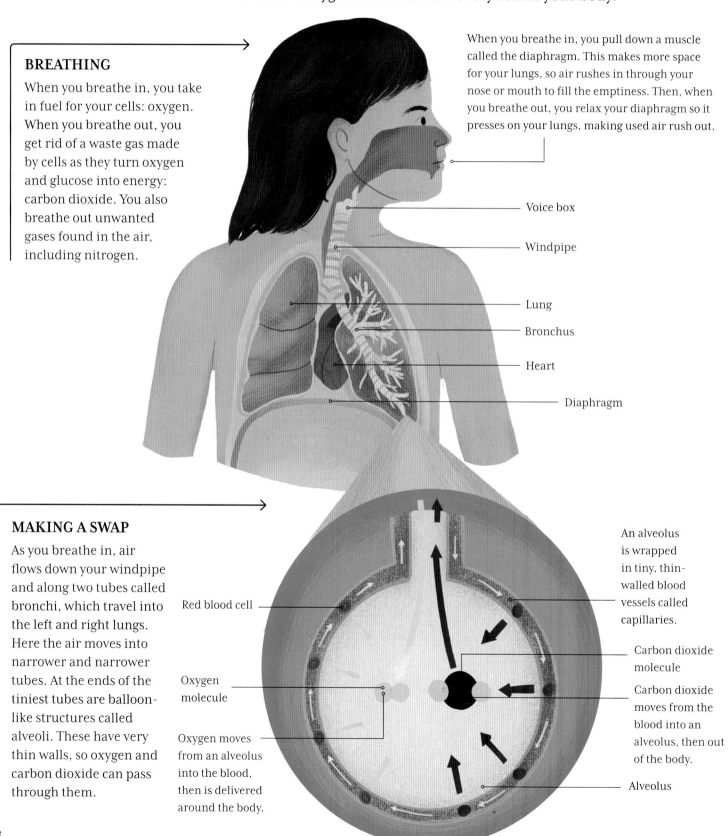

Voice box

Windpipe

Lung

Bronchus

Heart

Diaphragm

MAKING A SWAP

As you breathe in, air flows down your windpipe and along two tubes called bronchi, which travel into the left and right lungs. Here the air moves into narrower and narrower tubes. At the ends of the tiniest tubes are balloon-like structures called alveoli. These have very thin walls, so oxygen and carbon dioxide can pass through them.

Red blood cell

Oxygen molecule

Oxygen moves from an alveolus into the blood, then is delivered around the body.

An alveolus is wrapped in tiny, thin-walled blood vessels called capillaries.

Carbon dioxide molecule

Carbon dioxide moves from the blood into an alveolus, then out of the body.

Alveolus

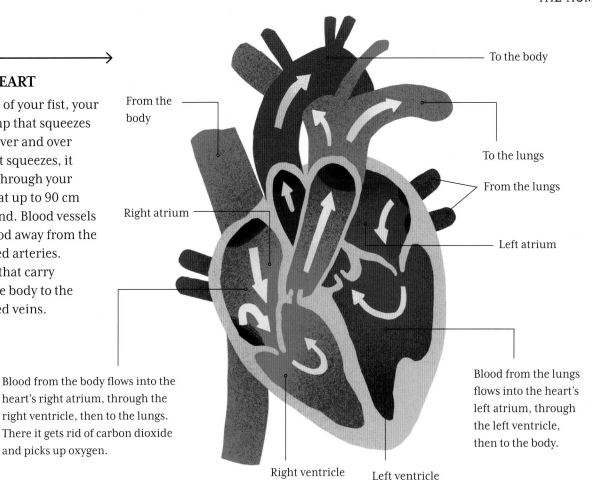

BEATING HEART

About the size of your fist, your heart is a pump that squeezes and relaxes, over and over again. When it squeezes, it shoots blood through your blood vessels at up to 90 cm (3 ft) per second. Blood vessels that carry blood away from the heart are called arteries. Blood vessels that carry blood from the body to the heart are called veins.

From the body

To the body

To the lungs

From the lungs

Right atrium

Left atrium

Blood from the body flows into the heart's right atrium, through the right ventricle, then to the lungs. There it gets rid of carbon dioxide and picks up oxygen.

Blood from the lungs flows into the heart's left atrium, through the left ventricle, then to the body.

Right ventricle   Left ventricle

IN YOUR BLOOD

Your blood is made of a pale-yellow liquid called plasma, in which are floating lots of red blood cells, white blood cells, platelets, nutrients from food, and waste.

Red blood cells carry oxygen to cells, where they pick up carbon dioxide to take to the lungs.

White blood cells help your body fight infection.

Platelets clump together if you cut yourself, making a scab and stopping your bleeding.

Scientist Profile

NAME   Christiaan Barnard
DATES   1922–2001
NATIONALITY South African
BREAKTHROUGH
In 1967, he carried out the first heart transplant: During surgery, a heart from a person who had just died was placed in the body of a patient with a diseased heart.

Digestive System

This organ system digests the food you eat: It breaks it down into basic parts, which can be transported and used by the body. The bits of food that your body cannot digest are expelled— as poop! It takes 1 to 3 days for food to travel from your mouth to the toilet.

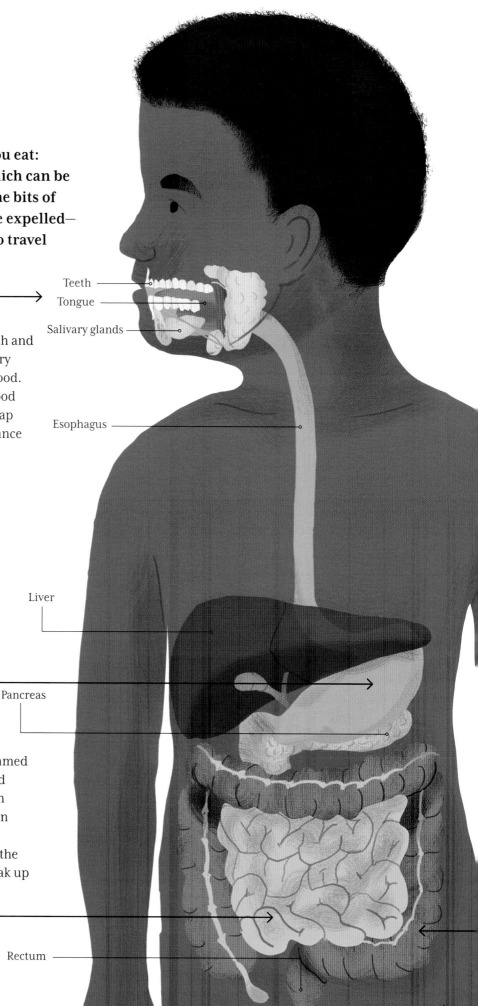

Teeth

Tongue

Salivary glands

Esophagus

Liver

Pancreas

Rectum

MOUTH

Food is sliced by your sharp front teeth and ground by your flat back teeth. Salivary glands release saliva (spit) to soften food. As you swallow, your tongue moves food toward your throat, and you close a flap called the epiglottis to block the entrance to your windpipe (see page 68).

STOMACH

Swallowed food enters a tube called the esophagus, which squeezes food toward the stomach. Your stomach is a muscly bag, which tightens and relaxes to churn food. The stomach's walls make acid, which kills some bacteria, and chemicals called enzymes that break food up.

SMALL INTESTINE

When food is soupy, it trickles through a ring of muscle into the small intestine. Named for its narrowness, this intestine is around 2.5 cm (1 in) wide but 4 m (13 ft) long in an adult. Here food is broken down by a green liquid called bile, made by the liver, and more enzymes, made by the pancreas. As the intestine squeezes food along, its walls soak up nutrients and pass them into the blood.

FOODS YOU NEED

If you are eating a variety of foods, including plenty of vegetables and fruits, your body is probably getting everything it needs to be healthy. A varied diet includes three types of foods: carbohydrate, protein, and fat. Enzymes in your digestive system break down these foods into essential nutrients.

Healthy fat is found in vegetable oils, nuts, seeds, and fish. It is broken into fatty acids and glycerol, which help your body store energy and make materials.

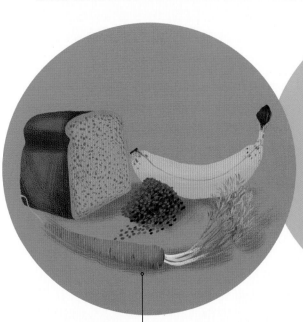

Healthy carbohydrate is found in whole grains (foods containing entire seeds, such as brown rice and whole wheat bread), vegetables, fruits, and beans. It is broken down into glucose, which is used by cells to make energy.

Healthy protein is found in fish, poultry, beans, nuts, cheese, and eggs. It is turned into amino acids, which are used for building new cells.

LARGE INTESTINE

The large intestine is around 7.5 cm (3 in) wide and 1.5 m (4.9 ft) long. Its walls soak up some water and the last nutrients. The large intestine's final section is called the rectum: This is where poop is stored until you go to the toilet.

Scientist Profile

NAME   Marie Maynard Daly

DATES   1921–2003

NATIONALITY: American

BREAKTHROUGH

She discovered the effects of eating saturated fats, which are found in animal-based foods such as red meat and eggs. The body needs fats to build healthy cells, but in very large amounts saturated fats can cause arteries to clog up, causing heart problems in older people.

A New Life

Your story began when you were a single cell, just 0.01 cm (0.004 in) across. Over the next nine months, maybe a little more or less, you developed into a beautiful newborn baby. A newborn has around 26 billion cells and is about 50 cm (20 in) long.

1 MINUTE

Most women release an egg from one of their ovaries every month. If an egg meets a man's sperm, the egg is fertilized, which means it is ready to grow into a baby.

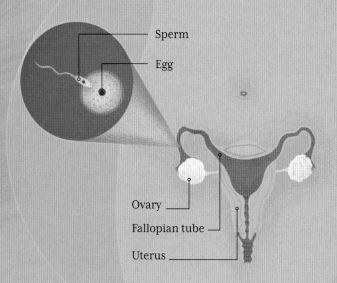

Sperm

Egg

Ovary

Fallopian tube

Uterus

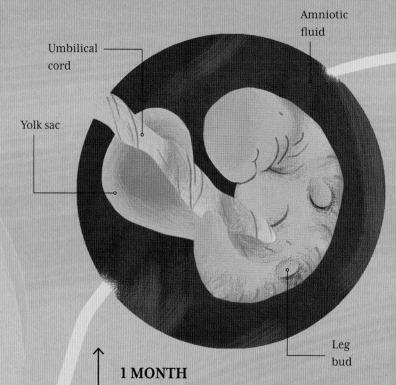

Amniotic fluid

Umbilical cord

Yolk sac

Leg bud

1 MONTH

The developing baby is the length of a grain of rice. It is now floating in a bag filled with liquid, called amniotic fluid, which will cushion it throughout pregnancy. The umbilical cord is taking shape: It will deliver nutrients and oxygen from mother to baby. Until the cord is ready, a pouch called the yolk sac supplies the baby with nutrients.

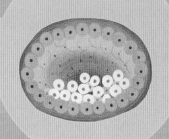

7 DAYS

The fertilized egg cell has split in two, over and over again, making around 120 cells. An inner group of cells will develop into the baby, while an outer group will make the structures that protect it during pregnancy. The cluster of cells has journeyed down the fallopian tube and into a stretchy organ called the uterus. It has burrowed into the uterus wall so it can soak up nutrients.

The average pregnancy lasts around nine months, but not every pregnancy is average. Pregnancies with twins—or triplets or more—are usually slightly shorter. Identical twins happen when a single egg develops into two similar-looking babies with nearly the same DNA (see page 36). Non-identical twins happen when a woman releases two eggs in one month, and each is fertilized.

Some parents need help from a doctor to get started with having a baby. The doctor may use a technique called in vitro fertilization (IVF), which is when the egg is fertilized with sperm in a laboratory, then placed in the woman's uterus to develop. Since the first IVF baby in 1978, more than 12 million heathy babies have been born using this method.

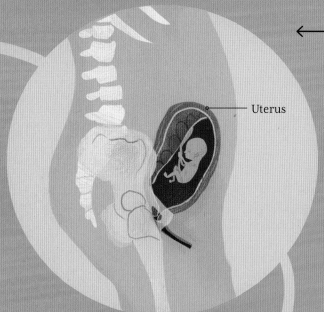

Uterus

4 MONTHS

Around the size of an avocado, the growing baby now has arms, fingers, legs, and toes. Its organs have formed, although most are not yet ready to function outside the safety of the uterus. The mother may start to feel her baby stretching and kicking, which helps its bones and muscles grow strong.

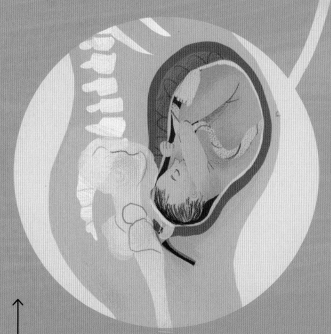

9 MONTHS

Most babies have turned head down ready for birth, as their smooth, round head will travel more easily down their mother's birth canal. The baby's lungs are strong enough to breathe air, while its stomach is ready to drink its mother's milk.

Medicine

**Medicine is the science of preventing, curing, or easing disease or injury.
Healthcare professionals, including doctors and nurses, train for several years.
They can work in many specialized areas, from surgery to infectious diseases.**

PRIMARY CARE

Primary care doctors and nurses diagnose and treat common illnesses. When diagnosing, they may examine the patient and ask about symptoms, which are features—such as a sore throat—that could be signs of illness. When necessary, primary care doctors send patients to specialist doctors or other healthcare professionals, such as therapists who help with speech or movement.

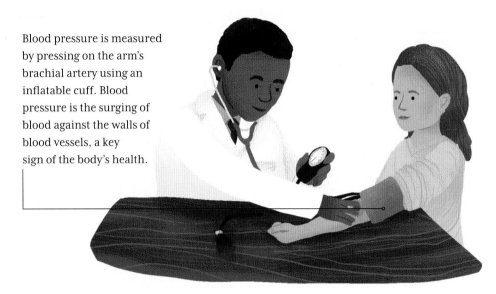

Blood pressure is measured by pressing on the arm's brachial artery using an inflatable cuff. Blood pressure is the surging of blood against the walls of blood vessels, a key sign of the body's health.

Cancer cells under a microscope

Normal cells

PATHOLOGY

Pathologists specialize in diagnosing disease, often by using a microscope to examine samples of tissue, blood, or urine. They may spot diseases such as cancer, which is when abnormal cells grow and reproduce uncontrollably, until doctors remove or destroy them.

Surgical tools, including scissors, scalpels, and tweezers, are cleaned so they are sterile, which means they are entirely free from living things.

SURGERY

A surgeon uses tools to reach into a patient's body to treat disease, mend injuries, or replace or remove damaged tissues and organs. Surgeons are helped by a team including a surgical nurse and an anesthetist (also called an anesthesiologist), a doctor trained to deliver anesthetics, which remove a patient's feeling or awareness for a short time.

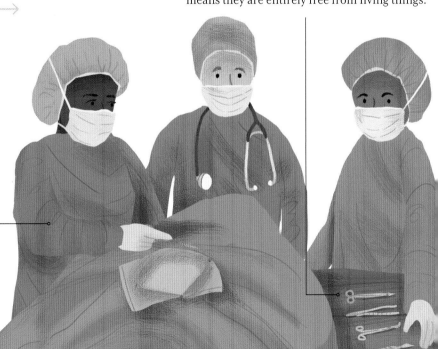

The surgical team wear clean masks, gloves, and gowns to stop bacteria or other tiny living things from infecting the patient.

PREVENTIVE MEDICINE

This branch of medicine aims to prevent disease, before patients become unwell. Methods include encouraging people to eat healthy food, to exercise, and not to smoke. Tests for common diseases are offered, as well as immunizations that prevent certain diseases.

An immunization teaches the body's lymphocytes (see "Lymphatic System" page 61) to recognize and destroy a certain bacteria or virus, often by injecting weakened or killed examples of it in a vaccine. This makes a person immune to a particular disease, so they will not get seriously ill if they are infected.

Scientist Profile

NAME   Edward Jenner
DATES   1749–1823
NATIONALITY   British
BREAKTHROUGH
He created the world's first vaccine, against the disease smallpox, using pus from blisters caused by cowpox, a similar but less deadly virus. The word vaccine comes from the scientific name for cowpox: vaccinia.

RADIOLOGY

Radiology uses imaging to see disease and injury inside the body. For example, ultrasound uses sound waves (see page 67) that are too high-pitched for humans to hear, bouncing the waves off organs to build up a picture. Medical resonance imaging (MRI) uses magnets to pull harmlessly on the body's protons (see page 8) so they line up. Protons in different cell types move at different speeds, creating an image that shows different tissues.

X-ray (see page 86) imaging is often used to see broken bones. This X-ray shows breaks in the tibia (shin bone) and fibula (calf bone). X-rays pass through skin and flesh, but they are absorbed by bones, creating lighter areas on the image.

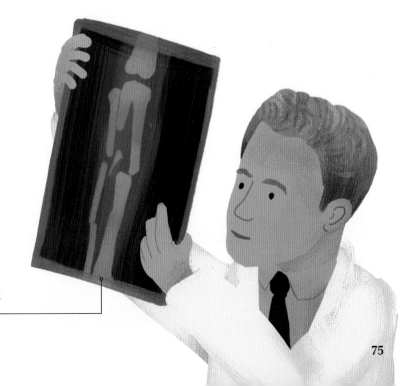

Forces and Energy

Without forces, the Universe would not exist. Any push or pull on an object or particle is a force. Forces such as the electromagnetic force help to hold together atoms by pulling together their tiny electrons and protons. Without atoms, there would be no matter: no planets or people. On a larger scale, forces are responsible for matter having the form we know and take for granted. Without the force of gravity, you would float off Earth into space—and, in fact, Earth would not exist to float away from. Forces including the reaction force stop you being able to put your hand through tables, walls, and people.

In our everyday lives, we use forces—pushes, pulls, and presses—to get everything done, from squeezing toothpaste on a brush to kicking a ball. You can see forces at work as they change the speed, direction, or shape of objects. When a force moves or changes the shape of an object, that is called work. Work changes energy from one form to another or transfers energy from one object to another. When you squeeze toothpaste or kick a ball, you are doing both. You are changing energy in your muscles into movement energy in the toothpaste or ball. You are also transferring energy from you to the toothpaste or ball. Energy is the ability to do work—the ability to apply a force that moves or changes the shape of an object.

Without energy, the Universe as we know it could not exist. Without energy, there could be no movement, change—or life. Energy takes many different forms, from the light we see to the mechanical energy of a speeding train. From humans' earliest days, we have learned to harness energy so we can eat, travel, and communicate. Hundreds of thousands of years ago, we learned to harness the chemical energy in wood by burning it, which releases heat energy that cooks food. Over the last few hundred years, we have learned to harness electrical energy to power light bulbs, machines, and televisions.

When you kick a soccer ball, you are applying a force. You are transferring energy from yourself to the ball. When the ball moves into the air, you have done work!

Born in the region of modern Iraq, Ibn al-Haytham (c.965–1040) was the first to explain that it is light reflecting off objects, into our eyes, that allows us to see. He realized this when he saw light shining through a tiny hole into his darkened room, projecting an image onto the opposite wall, as happens on the eye's retina. Light is a form of electromagnetic energy.

Forces at Work

Forces are pushes and pulls. We cannot see forces, but we can see their effects on objects. Forces make objects move, speed up, slow down, change direction, or change shape. Forces are caused by interaction between objects—when an object affects another object.

There are two types of forces: contact and non-contact. Contact forces act on objects when they are touching. Every day, you probably come across contact forces including tension, friction, spring, reaction, and applied forces.

Non-contact forces act between objects when they are not touching. These include gravity, as well as electric and magnetic forces (see page 93). Forces are measured in newtons, named after Sir Isaac Newton (see page 80): 1 newton is the force needed to accelerate (speed up) a 1 kg (2.2 lb) object by 1 m (3.3 ft) per second per second.

APPLIED

An applied force is a force applied to an object by a person or another object. If you push, pull, lift, or throw an object, you are applying a force to it. Scientists define "work" as the use of force to move an object. The farther the object is moved, the greater the work done.

FRICTION

Friction is a force between objects that are moving against one another, for example when a rabbit hutch is pushed across the floor. Friction works in the opposite direction from the way an object is moving, slowing it down. The rougher the surfaces, the greater the friction. A type of friction, called air resistance, acts between a moving object and the air, slowing the moving object.

GRAVITY

Gravity pulls all objects toward each other. The greater the mass (often called "weight") of an object, the bigger the pull of its gravity, so Earth's gravity is greater than a ball's. If you throw a ball upward, its speed slows due to Earth's gravity, which pulls in the opposite direction from the ball's motion. Finally, the ball stops, then falls to Earth—speeding up again as it plummets.

TENSION

This force travels through a rope or wire that is pulled tight. An acrobat dangling from a trapeze has tension exerted on them by the trapeze's rope. A team of sled dogs also pulls a sled using tension: The force travels through their harnesses and ropes.

REACTION

When an object rests on a surface, the surface pushes back with an equal force, known as the reaction force. So when a gymnast handstands on a pedestal, the pedestal pushes back on the gymnast. The heavier the gymnast, the greater the force exerted by the pedestal.

SPRING

A spring is a coil that returns to its original shape when stretched or compressed (squeezed). An object that compresses or stretches a spring is acted on by a force that returns the spring to its original shape. If a spring is compressed by an acrobat jumping on a springboard, the spring force pushes in the opposite direction—so the acrobat bounces into the air.

Laws of Motion

In 1687, the English scientist Sir Isaac Newton figured out three laws of motion. His three rules describe the relationship between the forces acting on an object and the way the object moves. The laws apply to objects bigger than an atom, on Earth and in space.

FIRST LAW OF MOTION

This law states that an object that is not moving will continue to not move, unless it is acted on by a force. It also states that an object that is in motion will stay in motion with the same speed and direction, unless it is acted on by a force. This law is one of the reasons why you must wear a seatbelt in a moving car: If the car brakes suddenly, you will keep on moving forward, unless you are restrained by a seatbelt.

A soccer ball does not move, unless a force acts on it.

The applied force of a kick sends a soccer ball into the air.

The soccer ball would continue to travel at the same speed and in the same direction, but the forces of gravity and air resistance act on it, bringing it to a stop on the ground.

SECOND LAW OF MOTION

The second law explains an object's acceleration, which is the rate at which it either speeds up or slows down. Newton explained that acceleration depends on the force acting on the object and the mass (often called "weight") of the object. If you double the force on an object, you double its acceleration. However, if you double the mass of an object, you halve its acceleration. This explains why it takes more force to move a heavy object than to move a light one.

Newton's second law tells us why it is harder work to push a full shopping cart than to push an empty one.

Scientist Profile

NAME	Isaac Newton
DATES	1643–1727
NATIONALITY	English

BREAKTHROUGH

In 1666, before figuring out the laws of motion, Newton realized that a force attracts every object to every other object, explaining why an apple falls to Earth. He called the force gravity (from the Latin *gravitas*, meaning "weight").

THIRD LAW OF MOTION

Newton's third law tells us that, for every action, there is an equal and opposite reaction. This means that forces come in pairs: When one object exerts force on a second object, the second object exerts an equal force on the first object. The third law explains how you skateboard on level ground: As you push off against the ground with your foot, the force of your kick is matched by the force the ground exerts on your foot—which propels you forward.

The third law explains how a rocket lifts off. Its engines burn fuel, creating a downward blast of hot gas—and an opposite force, which shoots the rocket upward.

Simple Machines

A machine is a device that uses forces to perform a task. These six simple machines were invented thousands of years ago. They make work easier by changing the strength or direction of a force. Many of today's complex machines, found in factories and vehicles, contain several of these simple machines.

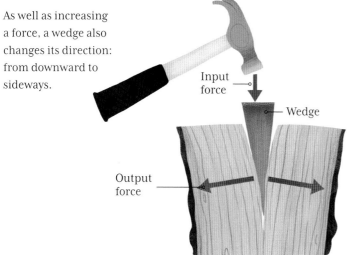

As well as increasing a force, a wedge also changes its direction: from downward to sideways.

Input force

Wedge

Output force

WEDGE

A wedge is a triangular block. This shape means that the force applied to the wedge is less than the resulting force. If a wedge is used to split wood, the applied force is a blow across the wedge's broader side. At the sharp end of the wedge, the force is concentrated in a smaller area, making the resulting force on the wood greater. You can see wedges in tools such as axes and shovels.

INCLINED PLANE

Also called a ramp, an inclined plane is a sloping surface. It takes less force to push a heavy box up a slope than it does to lift the box to the same height, because the slope supports some of the box's weight as it is pushed. However, you do need to move the box a greater distance, all the way up the long slope.

An inclined plane makes it easier for a wheelchair-user to reach a higher floor.

Inclined plane

Input force

Output force

WHEEL

It is much easier to pull a heavy box on a wheeled cart than to pull the box along the ground, since there is less friction (see page 78) between the narrow edge of the wheel and the ground than between a box and the ground. The bigger the wheels on the cart, the farther the cart travels without you having to pull harder.

An axle is the central rod around which a wheel turns.

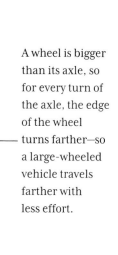

A wheel is bigger than its axle, so for every turn of the axle, the edge of the wheel turns farther—so a large-wheeled vehicle travels farther with less effort.

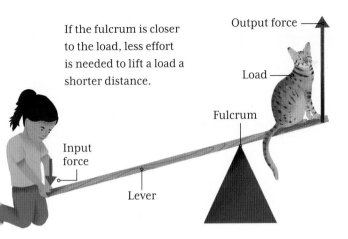

If the fulcrum is closer to the load, less effort is needed to lift a load a shorter distance.

Output force

Load

Fulcrum

Input force

Lever

LEVER

A lever is a straight rod or beam that can be pivoted (turned) around a turning point, called the fulcrum. If the fulcrum is closer to one end of the lever than the other, a lever makes it easier to lift a load. You must apply a downward force to the long end of the lever to lift a load resting on the opposite end. You press your end of the lever a greater distance to lift the opposite end a short distance, but this results in a greater lifting force on the load. You can see levers in wheelbarrows, scissors, and nutcrackers.

PULLEY

This simple machine is a wheel with a rope or cable looped around its rim. A pulley changes the direction of a force. If a load is attached to one end of the rope, pulling downward on the opposite end of the rope will lift the load upward.

Pulleys are often used by construction workers.

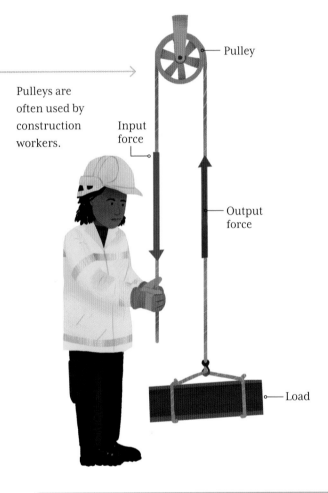

Pulley

Input force

Output force

Load

SCREW

A screw is a sharp-tipped pole with a spiraling groove, called a thread, around its edge. A screw changes a gentle turning force into a strong forward force. Less strength is needed to twist a screw into wood than to bang in a nail, because the screw spreads your effort over a longer distance—all the way along the edge of the spiral.

Output force

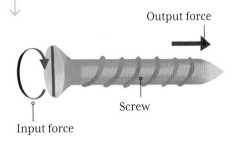

Screw

Input force

Each turn of the screw produces only a tiny movement of the screw tip into wood, so the work takes longer but requires less strength than banging in a nail.

Scientist Profile

NAME   Elisha Otis

DATES   1811–61

NATIONALITY American

BREAKTHROUGH
In 1852, he invented the safety elevator, which uses a system of pulleys and weights to carry passengers from floor to floor. He devised a safety brake to stop the elevator from falling if its cable breaks.

Energy

**Without energy, living things could not grow, and objects could not move.
Energy is the ability to do work, from climbing steps to blasting a rocket into space.
Energy cannot be created or destroyed, but it can be changed from one form to another.
There are two main types of energy: potential and kinetic.**

POTENTIAL ENERGY

Potential energy is stored energy. It could be released later
as kinetic energy. Everything holds potential energy.

NUCLEAR

This form of potential energy is stored inside the
nucleus of atoms (see page 28). Nuclear energy
holds the protons and neutrons in the nucleus
together. It can be released when nuclei split or
join together.

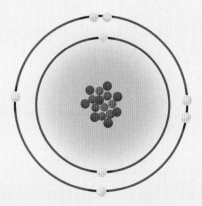

CHEMICAL

Chemical energy is stored in the bonds between
groups of atoms, called molecules. It can be released
when molecules undergo a chemical reaction (see page
22), breaking their bonds. Your body uses chemical
reactions to release the energy in food molecules.
The energy in fuels such as wood is released by a
combustion reaction, also known as burning.

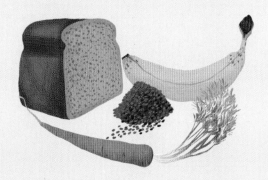

GRAVITATIONAL

This energy is stored in an object that could fall from a
height, due to the force of gravity. It can be released—
as mechanical energy—if the object falls. Usually, work
must be done to give gravitational potential energy
to an object: If you lift a bowling ball to a high shelf,
chemical energy stored in your muscles is changed
into gravitational potential energy.

ELASTIC

Elastic potential energy is stored inside an elastic
object—such as a spring, bowstring, or rubber
band—that has been stretched or squeezed. It can
be released as mechanical energy by
letting go of the object, so it
springs back into shape.
Work must be done to give
elastic energy to an
object, by pulling or
pressing it.

84

KINETIC ENERGY

Kinetic energy is the energy of motion. It is the energy an
object or particle has due to its movement.

MECHANICAL

This is the energy of objects in motion.
A plummeting rollercoaster, flowing
river, and turning windmill all
have mechanical energy. An object
with mechanical energy
can do work: It can apply a
force to move an object.
For example, a moving
hammer can bang in a nail.

THERMAL

Thermal energy is the movement of atoms.
All atoms are moving: slowly if they
are cool, but fast if they are hot
(see page 20). If something
has a lot of thermal energy,
it feels hot. The Sun is the
most powerful source of
thermal energy in our
Solar System.

RADIANT

Also known as electromagnetic radiation (see
page 86), this energy travels through space in the
form of waves. Radiant energy is given off by the
Sun and other stars, as well as by light bulbs.
It includes light, the only
form of energy that
can be seen by the
human eye.

SOUND

Sound energy is made when mechanical energy—
such as a drumstick hitting a drum—makes an
object vibrate (shake). Sound travels through the
air as a wave of vibrating molecules, a little like the
way a wave travels across the ocean.
This form of energy can be
heard by living things
(see page 67).

ELECTRICAL

Electrical energy is the movement of electrically
charged particles (see page 92). By powering
machines, heaters, light bulbs, and speakers,
electrical energy can be changed into mechanical,
thermal, radiant, or sound energy.

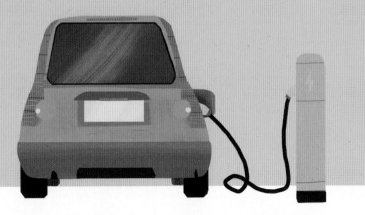

Electromagnetic Radiation

Electromagnetic radiation is the energy given off by the Sun and other stars. This energy travels through space as fast as anything can travel: 1,080,000,000 km/h (670,600,000 miles per hour), known as the speed of light. When the Sun's electromagnetic radiation reaches Earth, we feel some as heat and see some as light, but there are other forms that we can neither feel nor see.

RADIO WAVES

Radio waves have wavelengths between 30 cm and 100,000 km (12 in and 62,000 miles). As well as being released by the Sun, radio waves can be made by radio transmitters. These devices give waves particular patterns to carry information—sounds and images—for radios, televisions, computers, and phones.

MICROWAVES

Earth's atmosphere absorbs (soaks up) some of the Sun's energy with microwave wavelengths, between 1 mm and 30 cm (0.039 and 12 in), so much of it does not reach Earth's surface. Microwave ovens also make microwaves, which can travel into food, spinning molecules in the food—which heats them up and cooks the food.

INFRARED

Infrared wavelengths make up around half of the Sun's radiation that reaches Earth's surface. These wavelengths can be felt by humans as heat, because these photons are soaked up by the molecules they meet, making the molecules move faster (see page 20). Infrared wavelengths are used to send signals by remote controls for televisions and toys.

VISIBLE LIGHT

Photons with wavelengths between 0.0004 and 0.0007 mm (0.000016 and 0.00003 in) are the only things that human eyes can see (see page 66). You see objects because these photons bounce off

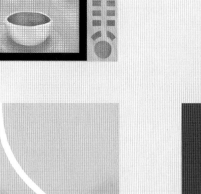

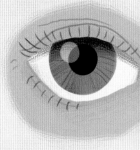

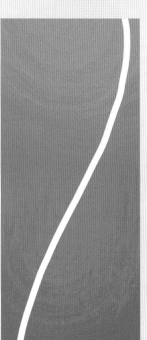

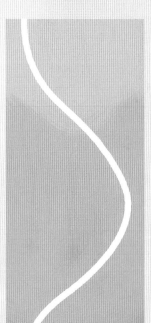

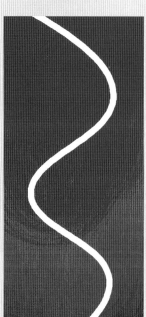

Electromagnetic radiation is made up of tiny particles called photons. Photons are packets of energy. This energy is "electromagnetic" because it is released by electrically charged particles: electrons and protons, which are found in atoms (see page 8). When atoms smash together in the core of the Sun (see page 116), their electrons release photons. These photons travel to the Sun's surface, then are released into space.

Electromagnetic radiation can behave both like a stream of photons and like a wave. Photons holding different amounts of energy have different wavelengths. Wavelength is the distance between the peaks of waves. The lowest-energy photons have the longest wavelengths. Different forms of electromagnetic radiation are made up of photons with different wavelengths, from low-energy radio waves to high-energy gamma rays.

them, then enter your eye through a hole called the pupil. The photons are absorbed by cells that cover the retina at the back of the eye, making the cells send electrical signals to your brain. Your brain makes sense of the signals, so you "see" the objects.

ULTRAVIOLET

This radiation can harm human skin, causing sunburn and permanent damage, so it is essential to wear sunscreen to protect yourself from the ultraviolet photons that are not absorbed by the atmosphere. Ultraviolet wavelengths are used in water treatment plants to kill bacteria and viruses in wastewater from toilets and baths.

X-RAYS

All X-rays are blocked by Earth's atmosphere. Medical X-ray machines produce photons that travel through the body and are absorbed in different amounts by different tissues. Those that pass out the other side create an image that shows the "shadows" made by different tissues. Doctors avoid X-raying too often, since repeated exposure can be harmful.

GAMMA RAYS

Most of these photons, with wavelengths less than 0.00000000000001 mm (0.0000000000000004 in), are blocked by Earth's atmosphere. They make atoms in living things give off electrons, which damages cells. Targeted gamma rays, given off by radioisotopes (see page 28), are used to kill cancerous cells, as well as microorganisms on medical equipment.

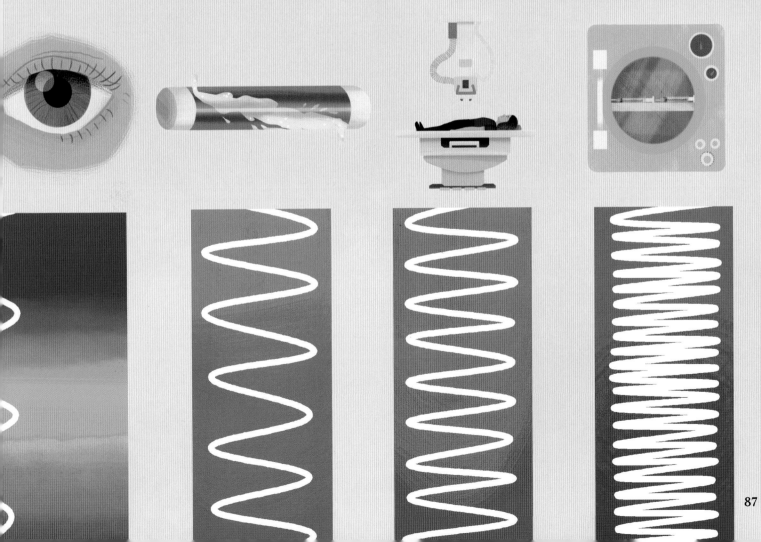

Light

Visible light is the form of electromagnetic radiation that humans can see. Without it, we would not be able to watch the world around us. On Earth, the main source of light is the Sun, but visible light is also given off by light bulbs, flames, and very hot objects.

THE SPECTRUM

The wavelength of visible light—the light that most humans can see—ranges from around 0.0004 to 0.0007 mm (0.000016 to 0.00003 in). Some animals can see a different range of electromagnetic radiation. For example, bees can see ultraviolet wavelengths as short as 0.0003 mm (0.000012 in). Flower petals have markings that can be seen only in ultraviolet light, which guide bees toward nectar.

Visible light is made up of all the colors of the rainbow: red, orange, yellow, green, blue, indigo, and violet. However, your eyes see the mixture of all these colors as white, which is why sunlight usually looks colorless. This range of colors is known as the spectrum. Each color is made of photons with a slightly different range of wavelengths, with red photons having the longest wavelengths and violet photons the shortest.

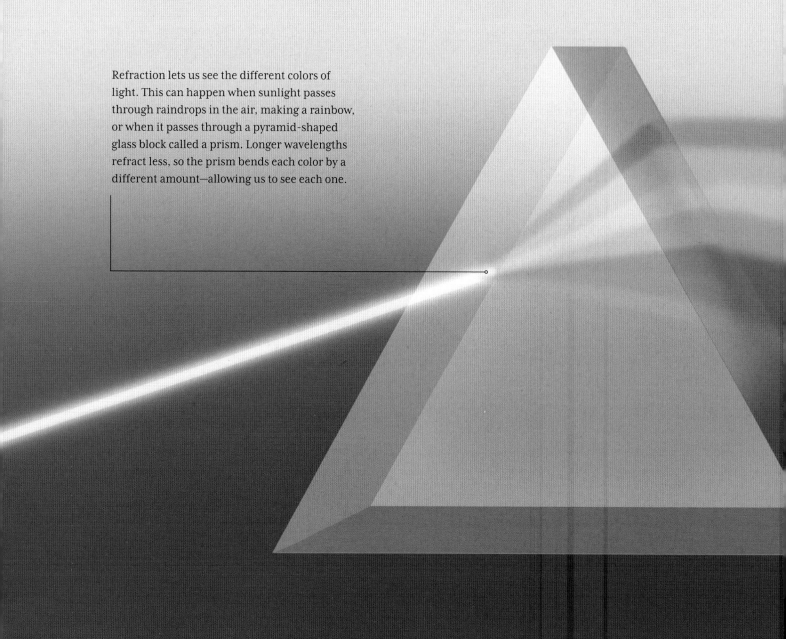

Refraction lets us see the different colors of light. This can happen when sunlight passes through raindrops in the air, making a rainbow, or when it passes through a pyramid-shaped glass block called a prism. Longer wavelengths refract less, so the prism bends each color by a different amount—allowing us to see each one.

WHAT WE SEE

Light travels in a straight line. It can pass through some materials, such as glass and water. These materials are known as transparent. Objects that light cannot pass through are known as opaque. They cast a shadow. Light reflects (bounces back) from them and into our eyes, so we can see them. Shiny materials, such as metal, reflect more light than rougher materials, such as rock, which absorb (soak up) more light.

Objects look different colors because of the way they absorb or reflect different wavelengths of light. When an object looks a particular color, that wavelength of light is being reflected into our eyes, while the other wavelengths are being absorbed.

BENDING LIGHT

When light enters a transparent material such as glass or water at an angle, it changes direction. This is known as refraction. It is caused by light slowing down as it enters a material that is denser (more tightly packed with molecules). Both glass and water are denser than air. This is why a drinking straw in a glass of water appears to bend where it enters the water.

It is easier to understand refraction if you imagine sunlight as a line of friends walking side by side into the ocean. If the line of friends meets the ocean at an angle rather than straight on, and each person slows down when they step into the water, one end of the line slows down before the other, so the line becomes crooked.

A red object absorbs all wavelengths except red, which it reflects into your eyes.

A white object reflects all wavelengths into your eyes, which see it as white.

A black object absorbs all wavelengths, so your eyes see it as black.

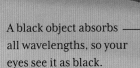

Scientist Profile

NAME	Ibn Sahl
DATES	c.940–1000
NATIONALITY	Persian

BREAKTHROUGH
In 984, he figured out the law of refraction. This is an equation that tells us how much light bends when it enters transparent materials.

Heat

You feel heat when you stand in the sunshine. But what is heat? Heat is thermal energy (see page 85) that is flowing from one object to another. Heat always flows from hotter objects to colder ones—making them warm up. As you warm up in sunshine, you feel heat!

HEAT OR TEMPERATURE?

We often use the words "heat" and "temperature" as if they mean the same thing. However, heat is a transfer of energy. Temperature is a measure of how much of that energy is in an object. The temperature of an object is determined by how fast its molecules are moving (see page 20). The faster they are moving, the higher the object's temperature.

Energy called heat flows from a hotter object to a colder one. As this happens, the molecules in the hotter object slow down and the molecules in the colder object speed up, until they reach the same temperature.

We measure temperature using the Kelvin (°K), Celsius (°C), or Fahrenheit (°F) scales. Heat can be measured in calories. A calorie is the energy needed to raise the temperature of 1 g (0.04 oz) of water by 1 °K (1 °C; 1.8 °F).

CONDUCTION

There are three ways that heat can transfer from one object or material to another. The first is conduction, which is how heat travels through solids; from a solid to a solid, liquid, or gas; or through liquids and gases that are not flowing.

In conduction, hot molecules or atoms vibrate or hit into colder molecules or atoms. Like balls that bounce into other balls, they pass on some of their movement: The colder molecules or atoms start to move faster, while the hotter molecules or atoms start to move slower.

Conduction happens more easily with solids, particularly metals, because their atoms are close together. Other materials—such as air—are poor conductors, since their molecules or atoms are widely spaced, so they bang into each other less. In fact, air is often used as an insulator: a material that stops heat conducting. Double-glazed windows often have a layer of air sandwiched between two pieces of glass to keep homes warm.

Scientist Profile

NAME	Josef Stefan
DATES	1835–93
NATIONALITY	Austrian

BREAKTHROUGH:

All objects radiate heat if their temperature is above absolute zero, the lowest possible temperature, which is 0 °K (-273 °C; -460 °F). Stefan figured out an equation that explains how the heat radiated by a hot object is greater than the heat radiated by a cool object.

CONVECTION

The second way that heat transfers is convection, which happens in liquids or gases that are moving. Convection is the rising motion of warmer areas of a liquid or gas, and the sinking motion of cooler areas. When a pan of water is heated on a stove, the water at the bottom of the pan is heated first. As this portion of the water's molecules speed up, they spread out, making it less dense. This less dense water rises, while the denser, cooler water at the top of the pan sinks, then is heated. This process repeats and repeats.

RADIATION

The third way that heat transfers is radiation, which can happen even when there is no solid, liquid, or gas to travel through. In radiation, heat travels as electromagnetic waves (see page 86) known as infrared.

When an infrared wave hits an object, heat energy is released, making its molecules move faster and so warming the object up. Radiate means "to spread out in all directions," just like heat travels from the Sun.

Conduction transfers heat through a spoon.

Radiation transfers heat from the Sun.

Convection transfers heat through soup.

Electricity

Electricity powers light bulbs, computers, and cars. Electricity is a form of kinetic energy: It is the movement of particles called electrons. The form of electricity that powers machines is called current electricity: It is a constant flow of electrons through an electric circuit.

MOVING ELECTRONS

As we discovered on page 8, the nuclei of atoms are orbited by particles called electrons, which have a negative electric charge. In nuclei are particles called protons, which have a positive charge. Like charges repel (push away), while opposite charges attract (pull): Positively and negatively charged particles attract each other, while two positively charged or two negatively charged particles repel.

A special type of force called the electromotive force (see "Electricity and Magnetism") can free an electron from its atom. Some types of materials—including metals such as copper—release electrons from their atoms more easily. These materials are called good conductors of electricity (see page 12). In a copper wire, it is quite easy to create a flow of electrons from atom to atom—an electric current.

MAKING A CIRCUIT

Electric current can flow through a circuit made of a loop of conducting material, such as a copper wire. Switching "on" a machine or light closes a circuit, allowing electrons to flow.

If we add a traditional light bulb to a circuit, electrons flow through the light bulb's filament, a thin wire made of a metal called tungsten. This makes the filament so hot that it glows, which changes electrical energy to thermal and light energy.

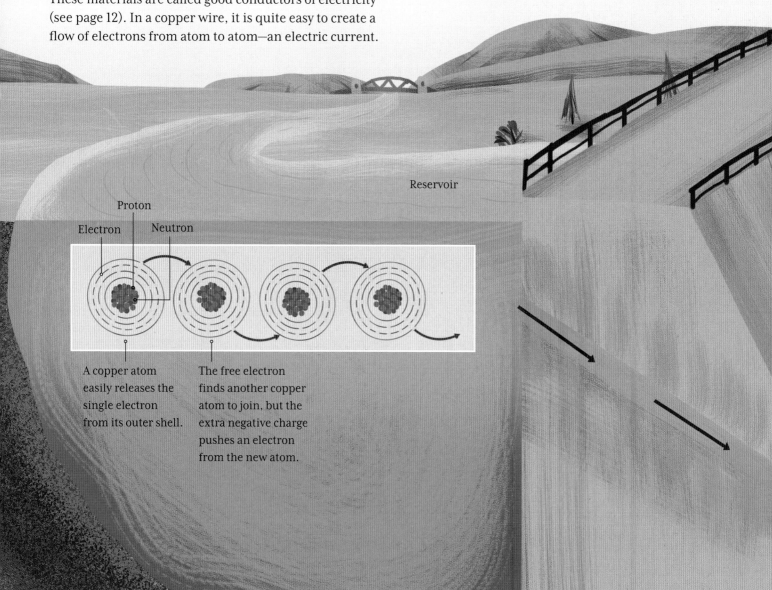

Reservoir

Proton

Electron   Neutron

A copper atom easily releases the single electron from its outer shell.

The free electron finds another copper atom to join, but the extra negative charge pushes an electron from the new atom.

ELECTRICITY AND MAGNETISM

Electricity and magnetism (see page 94) are two different but closely related things, both of them aspects of the electromagnetic force. Both electric and magnetic forces generate force fields (areas where their force can be felt), which repel objects with the same charge, or attract objects with the opposite charge.

The electric force acts between all electrons, whether or not they are moving. The magnetic force acts between moving electrons. A flow of electrons (electricity) can produce magnetism, while magnetism can produce electricity. We use this fact in electrical generators. Inside a generator, a coil of wire is spun inside a magnetic field. The magnetic field creates an electromotive force that makes electricity flow.

Scientist Profile

NAME	Michael Faraday
DATES	1791–1867
NATIONALITY	English

BREAKTHROUGH
He used a magnet and a coil of wire to create the first electrical generator, in 1831.

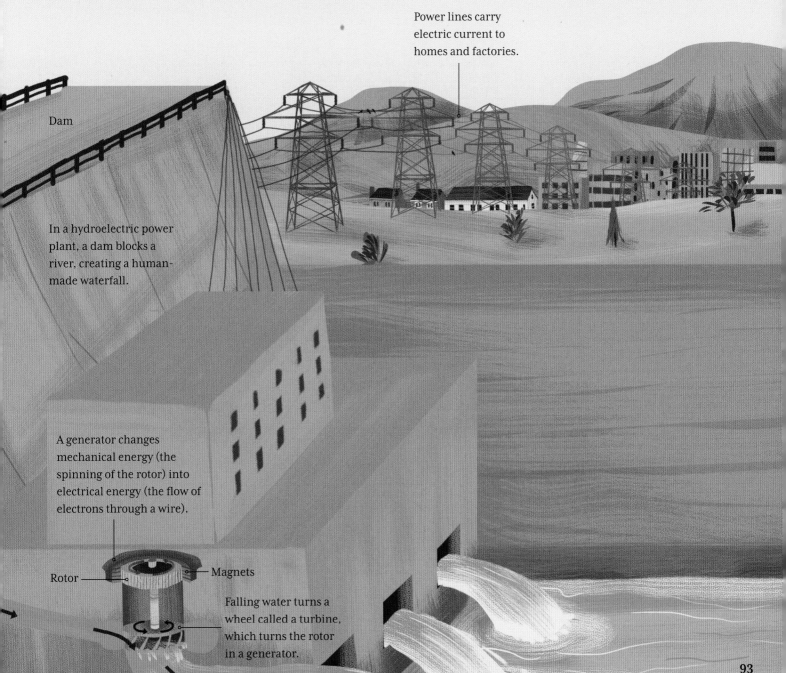

Power lines carry electric current to homes and factories.

Dam

In a hydroelectric power plant, a dam blocks a river, creating a human-made waterfall.

A generator changes mechanical energy (the spinning of the rotor) into electrical energy (the flow of electrons through a wire).

Rotor —— Magnets

Falling water turns a wheel called a turbine, which turns the rotor in a generator.

Magnetism

A magnet attracts and repels other magnets. It also attracts particular metals, such as iron, nickel, and cobalt. A magnet is surrounded by a magnetic field, an area where this force of attraction and repulsion can be felt.

WHAT IS A MAGNET?

A magnet is an object that has a magnetic field. Each magnet has a north pole and a south pole, which are two points on its surface where its surrounding magnetic field is strongest. Opposite poles attract, and like poles repel: The north and south poles of two magnets attract each other, while matching poles repel each other.

A maglev (short for "magnetic levitation") system uses magnets to propel a train. In China, Shanghai's maglev train runs at up to 430 km/h (267 miles per hour).

MAKING A MAGNET

A magnetic field is created by the spinning of particles called electrons (see page 92). Electrons act like tiny magnets. In most atoms, these tiny magnets come in pairs that spin in opposite directions so their magnetism cancels each other out. However, atoms such as those of the metals iron, nickel, and cobalt have a half-filled outer shell of electrons (see page 8), so all the electrons are unpaired—giving each atom a magnetic field. These metals are called ferromagnetic.

Yet all the electrons in all the atoms in a whole chunk of iron may not line up with each other, so a piece of iron is not necessarily a magnet. However, you can turn a ferromagnetic metal into a magnet by stroking it, in

one direction, with an existing magnet, making all its electrons line up. Together, all these tiny magnets produce a powerful magnetic force.

Magnets always attract ferromagnetic metals that have not already been turned into magnets. This is because the magnet pulls on the nearest unpaired electrons in the material, turning their unlike poles toward it—creating an attraction.

MAGNETIC EARTH

Earth is like a giant magnet due to the movement of electrons in the churning, molten iron that makes up much of its core (see page 106). Like all magnets, Earth has a north pole and a south pole. Compass needles are magnets that spin so they point toward Earth's magnetic north pole.

Scientist Profile

NAME	Francisca Nneka Okeke
BIRTH	1956
NATIONALITY	Nigerian

BREAKTHROUGH
She discovered how the Sun affects the electrojet, a river of electric current that circles Earth in the outer atmosphere. The electrojet is caused by electrons in the atmosphere moving in Earth's magnetic field.

The train is pushed and pulled forward by attraction and repulsion between magnets.

Repulsion between like poles levitates (raises) the train 10 cm (4 in) off the track to avoid friction.

Cars

The first successful car was invented in 1885. It could travel at 16 km/h (10 miles per hour). Today, there are nearly 1.5 billion cars on Earth. The very fastest of them can reach 1,228 km/h (763 miles per hour).

Petroleum-powered cars turn the chemical energy (see page 84) in oil into mechanical energy. They do this in an internal combustion engine, in which this liquid fuel is burned, producing hot gases that push down pistons, which turn a rod called a crankshaft, which turns the car's wheels. The problem with burning oil is that it releases the gas carbon dioxide, which worsens climate change (see page 112).

To fight against climate change, more and more cars are powered by electricity rather than oil. They contain a lithium-ion battery, which stores chemical energy in the bonds between its molecules. A chemical reaction (see page 22) changes the chemical energy into electrical energy by releasing electrons. This type of battery needs recharging—by supplying electrical energy that is stored as chemical energy—after driving up to 560 km (350 miles).

1959: VOLVO AMAZON

The three-point safety seatbelt was invented by Nils Bohlin, a Volvo car company employee. The Volvo Amazon was one of the first cars fitted with three-point seatbelts—attached to the car at the passenger's shoulder and on either side of the lap—as standard.

1885: BENZ PATENT-MOTORWAGEN

This was the first practical car and the first put into production: Around 25 were built. Invented by German engineer Carl Benz, it had an internal combustion engine and three wire and wooden wheels.

1908: FORD MODEL T

This was the first car built on a factory assembly line, where a car is constructed by a series of workers or machines as it moves along. Assembly lines made building cars cheaper and quicker, so more people could afford them. Powered by an internal combustion engine, the Model T reached 72 km/h (45 miles per hour).

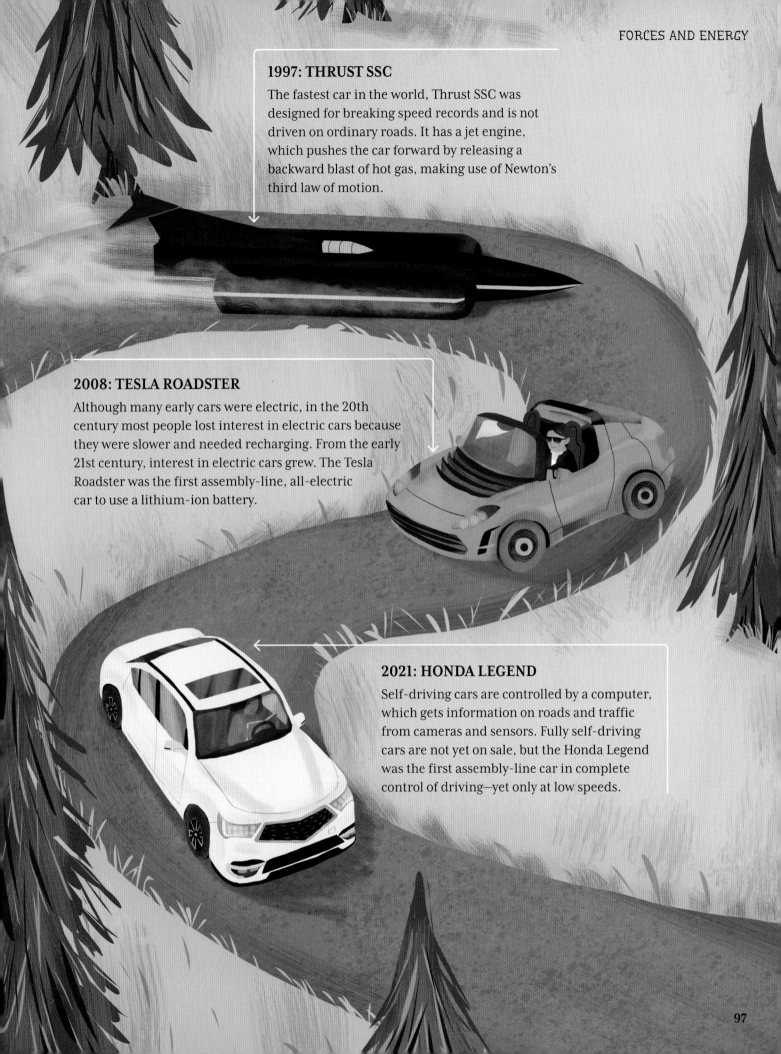

1997: THRUST SSC

The fastest car in the world, Thrust SSC was designed for breaking speed records and is not driven on ordinary roads. It has a jet engine, which pushes the car forward by releasing a backward blast of hot gas, making use of Newton's third law of motion.

2008: TESLA ROADSTER

Although many early cars were electric, in the 20th century most people lost interest in electric cars because they were slower and needed recharging. From the early 21st century, interest in electric cars grew. The Tesla Roadster was the first assembly-line, all-electric car to use a lithium-ion battery.

2021: HONDA LEGEND

Self-driving cars are controlled by a computer, which gets information on roads and traffic from cameras and sensors. Fully self-driving cars are not yet on sale, but the Honda Legend was the first assembly-line car in complete control of driving—yet only at low speeds.

Computers

Most people use a computer every day, when doing homework on a laptop or searching the web on a smartphone. A computer is a machine that works with information. For computers to use information easily, all words, numbers, pictures, and sounds are turned into a simpler form: just 0s and 1s.

DIGITAL DEVICES

Computers are digital, which means they work with digits (numbers): 0s and 1s. All information, which computer scientists call data, is turned into 0s and 1s by a computer. For example, the letter A becomes 01000001. Computers are powered by electricity. Inside a computer is a microprocessor, which contains billions of tiny electric circuits, which can be turned on and off by switches called transistors. A 0 turns a transistor off, but a 1 turns it on. Patterns of 0s and 1s turn these billions of circuits on and off in countless patterns, completing all a computer's work.

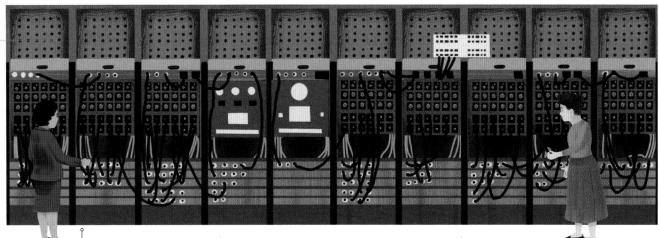

Built in 1945, ENIAC (Electronic Numerical Integrator and Calculator) was the first successful electronic digital computer. It had around 18,000 circuits, which were so large the computer was 30 m (100 ft) long.

PROGRAMMING

A program is a set of instructions that tells a computer what to do in which order. We write programs in programming languages, such as C and Perl, in which commands are given by simple combinations of words and symbols—which can more easily be turned into 0s and 1s by a computer. A combination of programming and data makes software. Different pieces of software let you search the web, send emails, or paint pictures.

The first programmer was English mathematician Ada Lovelace (1815–52). However, she wrote programs for a machine that was never fully built: Charles Babbage's steam-powered, clockwork Analytical Engine.

THE WEB

The web is all the world's websites that you can access using the internet. The internet is a worldwide network—formed by wires, cables, and wireless links (see page 100)—through which computers send data. The web was invented by English computer scientist Tim Berners-Lee in 1989, when he created hypertext transfer protocol (HTTP). This sets out how websites are sent through the internet, from the computer where their data is stored to your computer, so you can see them.

There are more than 1 billion websites.

ROBOTS

Robots are machines that contain a computer, which instructs them to carry out actions. The first successful industrial robot, Unimate, was built in 1959. It was a moving arm on a factory assembly line. Today, we have robotic toys and traffic signals, as well as robots that help surgeons operate.

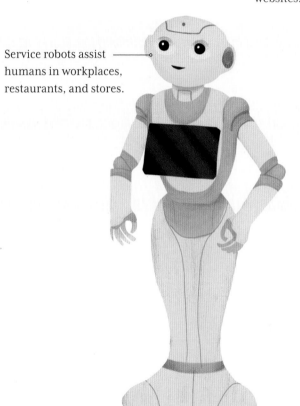

Service robots assist humans in workplaces, restaurants, and stores.

ARTIFICIAL INTELLIGENCE

Artificial intelligence (AI) is software that allows computers to perform complex tasks, such as solving problems or writing stories. Although AI software makes it seem as if computers are thinking for themselves, they are only following programs that instruct them how to choose between options. In addition, AI software includes lots of data to check against. For example, weed-spotting AI software, used by farming robots, includes lots of photos of weeds.

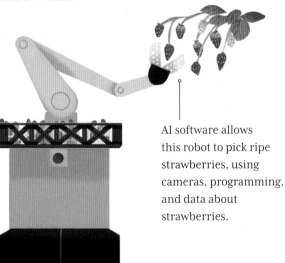

AI software allows this robot to pick ripe strawberries, using cameras, programming, and data about strawberries.

Scientist Profile

NAME	Alan Turing
DATES	1912–54
NATIONALITY	English

BREAKTHROUGH

In 1950, long before computers could run complex programs, he designed a test to judge how well a computer can mimic human thinking: A human asks questions—via a computer screen—to both a human and a computer, then guesses which is which.

Communication

Communication is how we send and receive information. Communication devices such as phones and televisions make use of radio waves and cables to receive sounds and pictures—so you can call a friend or watch the latest show.

USING RADIO WAVES

A huge breakthrough in communication took place in 1896, when Italian inventor Guglielmo Marconi became the first person to use radio waves to send a simple message. Today, when images or sounds are sent as radio waves, the information is usually first converted into a digital signal: a stream of 0s and 1s (see page 98). This pattern turns an electric current off (0s) and on (1s).

When an on-off electric current flows into a device called a radio transmitter, it makes electrons vibrate, which produces radio waves that travel through the air. The pattern of 0s and 1s is represented by the changing shape of the radio waves. When the waves reach a radio receiver—in a device such as a radio, phone, television, or computer—they are turned back into an electrical signal.

MAKING SOUNDS

In a radio, phone, or a television or computer's speakers, the electrical signal is turned into sound waves. To make this happen, the electric current passes through a coil of wire, creating a changing magnetic field. This attracts and repels a magnet attached to a cone of flexible material, making it vibrate. This vibration shakes the air—and the sound waves travel to your ears (see page 67).

MAKING IMAGES

Images and sounds are usually converted into a digital signal, then sent to televisions by underground cables or by radio waves, which travel directly from local transmitters or are reflected off communication satellites in orbit around Earth.

Some modern communication cables are not made of metal wire, which carries the signal as electrons, but of optical fiber. In these thin glass or plastic pipes, the signal travels as pulses of light. At the destination, the light signal is then converted into an electrical signal by a device known as a photodetector, which generates electricity when light falls on it.

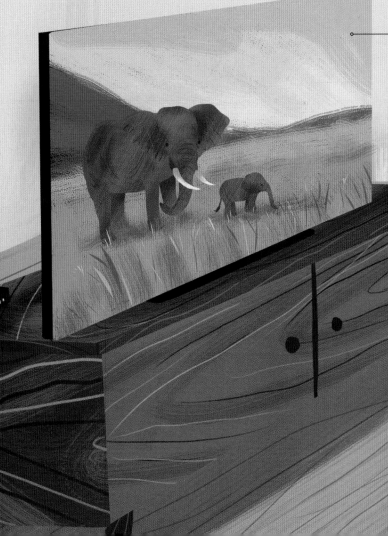

A wireless router sends and receives radio waves over a short distance, creating a local wireless network so people nearby can access the internet or send data between devices. A router is usually plugged into a wired network.

The picture on a television screen is made up by a grid of thousands of tiny dots, called pixels. Every pixel contains red, green, and blue subpixels that light up by different amounts, together creating the full spectrum of colors.

Different types of televisions turn the electrical signal into images in different ways. For example, in a plasma TV, each subpixel is a tiny light containing plasma (see page 18). Electric current flowing through the plasma makes it give off light. The signal turns on some subpixels but not others—and, together, the lit pixels create an image.

Scientist Profile

NAME   Hedy Lamarr
DATES   1914–2000
NATIONALITY: Austrian-American
BREAKTHROUGH
In 1942, this movie star invented the technique that would later be used for wireless networks such as Wi-Fi and Bluetooth. She created a transmitter-receiver system that constantly changed the frequency (number of waves per second) of radio waves, so messages could not easily be intercepted by anyone not allowed on the network.

When you call a friend, a cell phone (also called a mobile phone) sends radio waves to a local phone mast, which sends them on through a network of masts to the destination phone. If you call a friend overseas, your signal may travel part of the way through an undersea optical fiber cable.

The first television picture was transmitted in 1926 by Scottish inventor John Logie Baird.

Our Energy Sources

We harness energy to make electricity, power vehicles, heat and cool homes, and cook food. Sources of this energy fall into two types: renewable, which means they will never run out; and non-renewable—which means they will. Currently, around one-fifth of the world's energy comes from renewable sources.

Renewable energy sources include those created by natural processes, such as sunlight, wind, moving water, and geothermal heat. These sources have the extra benefit of not usually causing pollution. In addition, biomass sources—such as plants—are usually renewable, because they can be replanted. However, some biomass—such as wood—is not sustainable, which means it is being used at too great a rate to meet future needs.

Non-renewable sources include fossil fuels: coal, oil, and natural gas. Although fossil fuels were made by natural processes, they form too slowly to be considered renewable. It takes millions of years for them to form underground from dead animals and plants. Another problem with fossil fuels is that, when burned, they release carbon dioxide, which worsens climate change (see page 112). Nuclear energy (see page 29) is also non-renewable, as it uses rare elements that must be mined. However, if carried out carefully, harnessing nuclear energy does not create pollution.

WIND

In wind farms, the wind's mechanical energy turns turbine blades, which spins rotors in generators, which then make electrical energy. Wind farms are sited in windy places, such as hilltops and the coastal ocean.

WATER

The mechanical energy of falling or flowing water is harnessed in hydroelectric (see page 92) and tidal (pictured) power plants. Tidal energy uses tides—the rising and falling of sea levels due to the Moon's gravity—to turn turbines and spin rotors in electrical generators.

FOSSIL FUELS

Fossil fuels are dug or pumped from the ground, then burned in power plants to boil water into steam, which turns turbines that power electrical generators. Oil is also burned in vehicle engines. In homes, natural gas is burned to cook food and heat water for washing and heating systems.

BIOMASS

Biomass means "material from living things." In some countries, plants or animal waste are burned to cook food and heat homes. Biomass can also be burned in power plants to heat water. Plants such as sugarcane (pictured) are made into liquid fuel that is burned in some vehicle engines.

SUNLIGHT

Solar panels convert the Sun's radiant energy into electrical energy. On house roofs, solar thermal panels convert sunlight into heat, which warms water for washing and heating systems.

GEOTHERMAL HEAT

Geothermal means "Earth heat." In certain places, Earth's crust (see page 108) is so hot that it can heat water, which is used to make electricity or pumped into heating systems. In these systems, hot water flows in pipes to radiators, which heat rooms through convection and radiation.

Earth and Space

Earth is one of eight planets in orbit around the Sun, which is a super-hot sphere of gas known as a star. An orbit is a curving path around a star or planet. The Sun is by far the largest object in this region of space, with a thousand times the mass of its largest planet, Jupiter. Gravity is a force that pulls all objects toward each other, but more massive objects have greater gravity—so the pull of the Sun's gravity is felt by objects up to 30 trillion km (18.6 trillion miles) away. The eight planets formed from a spinning disk of material around the newborn Sun. They have continued their rotating journey ever since. With no other force to bring them to a stop, the Sun's gravity keeps the planets in their orbits.

Planets are large, rounded objects that orbit a star. They are large enough for their own gravity to pull them into a ball shape. While some—such as Earth—are made of rock and metal, others are made of flowing liquids and gases. In addition to the eight planets, other large objects are spinning around the Sun. Among them are dwarf planets, which are smaller than true planets, with gravity large enough to make them ball-shaped but not large enough to clear other big objects out of their orbit. There are also hundreds of moons, which are rounded objects held in orbit around a planet or dwarf planet by the planet's gravity.

The Sun is one of perhaps 100 billion stars in our galaxy, the Milky Way. Like the other 2 trillion galaxies in the known Universe, the Milky Way is a collection of stars, planets, gas, and dust. Most planets in the Milky Way are in orbit around a star. Since the average star is orbited by at least one planet, astronomers estimate that, in the whole Universe, there may be 1 septillion planets. In our Solar System, our planet is special, because it is the only one warm and watery enough to be home to life. Yet, in the vast Universe, there may be another planet—or even lots of planets—that are warm, watery, and home to extraordinary life.

The largest dwarf planet orbiting the Sun is Pluto, which is around 2,376 km (1,476 miles) across. It has five known moons. Since Pluto orbits the Sun at a great distance, around 5.9 billion km (3.7 billion miles) away, it is extremely cold, with an average surface temperature of -229 °C (-380 °F).

Although she lived at a time when most Chinese women were not allowed to study or to work outside the home, Wang Zhenyi (1768–97) educated herself in astronomy. Using a lantern (representing the Sun), table (Earth), and mirror (the Moon), she figured out a mathematical explanation for eclipses of the Moon, which is when the Moon passes into Earth's shadow.

Earth

Around 12,756 km (7,926 miles) wide, our planet is a sphere of rock and metal. It is spinning around the Sun, completing one journey—called an orbit—in just over 365 days. Earth has a companion on this journey: the Moon, which completes an orbit around Earth every 27.3 days.

Earth formed in a disk of spinning dust and gas.

FORMATION

Astronomers think that, around 4.6 billion years ago, a dusty cloud of hydrogen and helium gas was shaken by the explosion of a dying star. The cloud collapsed, forming a clump at its heart. The clump's gravity pulled in more and more material, until it became a glowing star: the Sun (see page 116). A disk of leftover material spun around the newborn Sun. Clumps formed in the disk, bumped into each other, and grew. The third clump from the Sun became Earth.

At first, Earth was a ball of mixed, molten metal and rock, heated to 10,000 °C (18,000 °F) by crashing and squeezing. Then the metals—which are heavier than rock—sank to Earth's core, while rock formed its outer layers.

The crash sent rock and metal shooting into space, where—held and shaped by Earth's gravity and its own—it formed an orbiting sphere: the Moon. As the Moon orbits Earth, it appears to change shape as different portions of its surface are lit by sunlight.

About 30 to 50 million years after Earth formed, it was probably hit by a small planet called Theia.

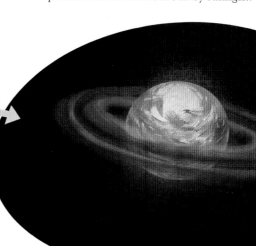

Young Earth's many volcanoes (see page 108) spewed out gases, which were held around the planet by its gravity, forming an atmosphere. By 4.4 billion years ago, Earth had cooled enough for rain (see page 110) to fall from clouds in the atmosphere, then collect in dips in the planet's surface, making oceans. It was in the oceans that life began, around 3.8 billion years ago.

STRUCTURE

Earth has four layers: the inner core, outer core, mantle, and crust. Its inner and outer core are metal, mostly iron and nickel. Earth has cooled since its formation, but it is still around 3,700 °C (6,700 °F) in the outer core. In this great heat, the metal is liquid. However, the metal in the still-hotter inner core is solid, because it is pressed so hard by all the surrounding material: The atoms are squeezed too tightly to separate into a liquid state (see page 20). With an average temperature of 2,000 °C (3,630 °F), the mantle is made of rock that has melted in places. The crust is lighter, solid rock. Its surface has an average temperature of 14 °C (57 °F), making it suitable for life.

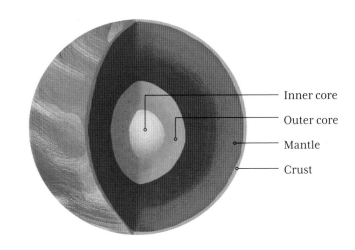

Inner core
Outer core
Mantle
Crust

ROTATION AND ORBIT

Earth rotates around its axis once every 24 hours. When one side of Earth faces the Sun, it has day, while the other has night. The collision that created the Moon probably also knocked Earth over, so it tilts by 23.5 degrees. This affects Earth's days and creates seasons: When one hemisphere (half) of Earth is tilted toward the Sun, it has summer, with longer, warmer days. For thousands of years, humans have watched the seasons, keeping pace using calendars. Yet since Earth takes 365.25 days to orbit, the modern calendar adds an extra day every fourth year, creating a "leap year" of 366 days.

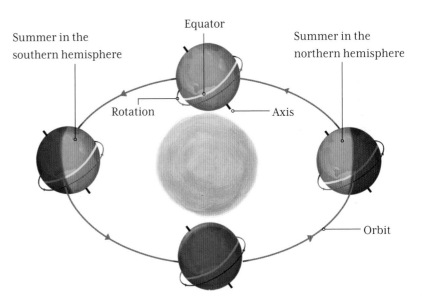

Summer in the southern hemisphere

Equator

Summer in the northern hemisphere

Rotation

Axis

Orbit

Like all orbits, Earth's is a stretched circle called an ellipse. In one orbit, our planet covers 940 million km (584 million miles).

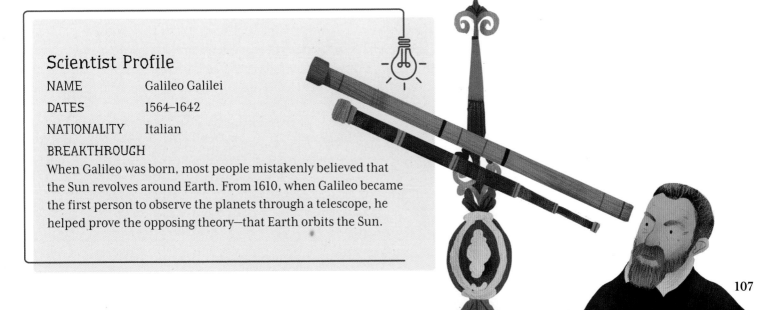

Scientist Profile

NAME   Galileo Galilei

DATES   1564–1642

NATIONALITY Italian

BREAKTHROUGH

When Galileo was born, most people mistakenly believed that the Sun revolves around Earth. From 1610, when Galileo became the first person to observe the planets through a telescope, he helped prove the opposing theory—that Earth orbits the Sun.

Earth's Crust

Earth's crust is between 5 and 70 km (3 and 43 miles) thick. The crust is broken into jagged-edged pieces, called tectonic plates, which float on the hot rock beneath. The movement of these plates creates mountains and deep crack-like valleys, as well as earthquakes and volcanoes.

MOVING PLATES

Around 3 billion years ago, as Earth cooled, the crust and upper mantle cracked into around seven large plates and many smaller ones. We cannot usually see the edges of plates at the surface because they are covered by soil, water, or new rock. However, the plates move by up to 10 cm (4 in) per year, as the partly melted rock in the mantle flows very slowly, rising and falling due to convection (see page 91). The movement of tectonic plates has reshaped Earth's continents many times over.

The edges of plates are called boundaries. There are three main types of boundaries. At convergent boundaries, the plates are moving toward each other. One plate sinks below the other, which folds or shoves rock upward, creating mountain ranges. At divergent boundaries, the plates are moving apart. This can create deep valleys called rifts. At transform boundaries, plates are sliding past each other.

Convergent boundary

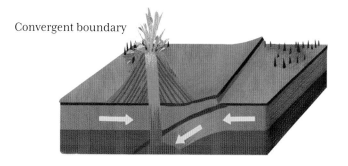

Divergent boundary

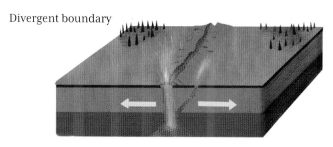

Transform boundary

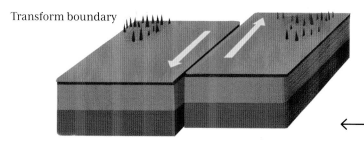

EARTHQUAKES

Earthquakes usually take place at plate boundaries. They can happen at any of the three boundary types, when the plates get stuck on each other as they move. Pressure builds until the rock suddenly cracks, shaking the ground. The shaking travels through the ground in waves, called seismic waves. Like ripples on a pond, these weaken as they spread outward.

The spot underground where the rock breaks is called the earthquake's hypocenter. The spot on the surface above the hypocenter is called the epicenter. Close to the epicenter, powerful earthquakes can damage buildings, roads, and power lines. Sometimes, if the epicenter is underwater, earthquakes make tall ocean waves called tsunamis.

VOLCANOES

Volcanoes are cracks in the crust where hot rock—called magma—escapes. Volcanoes often form at divergent and convergent boundaries. At divergent boundaries, magma wells up from the mantle between the two plates. At convergent boundaries, rock is melted, then surges to the surface. Volcanoes can also form in the middle of plates, over very hot areas in the mantle, called hotspots. Earth's largest volcano, Mauna Loa on the Island of Hawaii, formed over a hotspot in the Pacific Plate.

Once magma has erupted, it is called lava. Over time, many volcanoes take the shape of mountains as their lava cools into solid rock, eruption after eruption. Stratovolcanoes erupt thick lava that does not flow far before it cools, creating a tall cone shape. Shield volcanoes have runnier lava, which forms a flatter shape, like an ancient warrior's shield.

There are three main types of boundaries between tectonic plates. In each type, the plates are moving differently in relation to each other.

Ash cloud

Crater

Lava flow

Mount Etna is an active stratovolcano on
the Italian island of Sicily, which lies on a
convergent boundary. An active volcano is
either erupting or likely to erupt in the future;
a dormant volcano may possibly erupt again;
while an extinct volcano no longer has a
magma supply so cannot re-erupt.

Side vent

Crust

Magma chamber

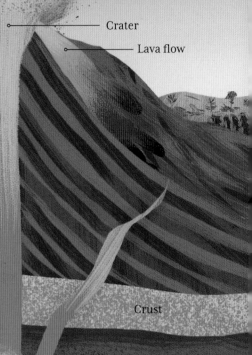

Scientist Profile

NAME   Inge Lehmann

DATES   1888–1993

NATIONALITY Danish

BREAKTHROUGH
Lehmann studied how seismic waves
travel through Earth. In 1936, her studies
made her the first to realize that our
planet must have a solid inner core within
its liquid outer core.

Upper mantle

The Water Cycle

The water cycle is the constant movement of water through Earth's air, across its surface, and underground. As water moves, it changes state: from liquid water, to solid ice, to gassy water vapor. In total, all Earth's water adds up to 1.4 billion cubic km (336 million cubic miles).

AROUND AND AROUND

The water cycle is driven by the Sun, which heats water in oceans, lakes, rivers, and ponds. Surface water evaporates (see page 21), turning from a liquid to an invisible gas, called water vapor. Water also evaporates from plant leaves and soil.

Water vapor rises in warm air: Since warm air has more space between its molecules than cool air, it is less dense—so it floats upward. As air rises, it cools. Cool air can hold less water vapor than warm air, so some water vapor condenses (see page 21) into water droplets. We can see clusters of these droplets as clouds.

When water droplets grow too big and heavy to float, they fall as rain. In cold weather, water may fall as joined ice crystals, called snow. Rain, snow, hail, and sleet are all types of precipitation, which is any form of water that falls to the ground.

Back on Earth, water makes many journeys. It may freeze in ice sheets at the poles or on mountaintops. It may flow to the ocean in rivers that travel above- or underground. Water may collect in lakes, reservoirs, or swamps; or in underground rock or soil, where it is known as groundwater.

Precipitation

Condensation

Evaporation

The water cycle is continuous: When water reaches Earth's surface, its cycle begins again.

ESSENTIAL CYCLE

As water evaporates, it leaves behind most of its impurities, such as salts. This is how the water cycle supplies land animals and plants with fresh, clean water, which they use to transport materials through their bodies. The water cycle also keeps oceans healthy, as the inflow of cool fresh water drives the mixing of ocean water—with cold water sinking and warm water rising—carrying nutrients and oxygen to all its living things.

In addition, the water cycle shapes Earth's surface. Over many years, rivers wear away rock and soil, carving wide valleys or narrow canyons. Bodies of ice, called glaciers, slide slowly down mountainsides, grinding out valleys with the boulders they carry.

Scientist Profile

NAME	Syukuro Manabe
BIRTH	1931
NATIONALITY	Japanese-American

BREAKTHROUGH
He pioneered the use of computers to create models of Earth's atmosphere and study how changing conditions affect weather. In 1966, he warned the world about climate change (see page 112).

CLOUDS

Different types of clouds form at different heights in Earth's atmosphere. Among the highest are cirrus clouds, which form at up to 20 km (12.4 miles) high from ice crystals. The lowest, known as fog or mist, form at ground level when cold air is very full of water vapor.

Thick, dark clouds tend to bring rain or snow, while high, wispy clouds do not.

Cirrus: High, wispy clouds formed when warm, dry air rises.

Cirrocumulus: High, puffy clouds of ice crystals and water droplets.

Nimbostratus: Dark, thick layers of cloud that often bring heavy precipitation.

Cumulonimbus: Tall thunderclouds formed when hot, wet air rises fast.

Cumulus: Low, white puffy clouds that do not usually bring rain.

Stratus: Low featureless clouds that may bring light rain.

Climate Change

When scientists talk about climate change, they mean the changes in Earth's weather over the last 30 to 50 years. Climate change is caused by a rise in the temperature of Earth's air and oceans. That temperature rise, known as global warming, is caused by human activities.

Three main human activities are causing global warming and climate change: burning fossil fuels, cutting down forests, and farming methods. These activities release greenhouse gases into the atmosphere. Greenhouse gases—including carbon dioxide, methane, and nitrous oxide—trap the Sun's heat, a little like the glass in a greenhouse, making Earth warmer.

Greenhouse gases have always been in the atmosphere, but the extra quantities we have released since 1880 have made Earth 1 °C (1.9 °F) hotter. If we let greenhouse gas emissions continue to rise at the current rate, by 2100, Earth might be 5 °C (9 °F) warmer than in 1880. However, governments, businesses, and ordinary people are working to reduce emissions so we can slow down climate change.

BURNING FOSSIL FUELS

Humans burn coal, oil, and natural gas (see page 102) in power plants, factories, homes, and vehicles. This releases carbon dioxide, as well as smaller amounts of methane and nitrous oxide. Burning fossil fuels causes three-quarters of greenhouse gas emissions.

DEFORESTATION

In some regions, forests are cut down to make room for farms, towns, and factories. Trees soak up carbon dioxide (see page 43), so deforestation means less carbon dioxide is absorbed from the air. Burning trees releases the carbon dioxide they have stored.

FARMING METHODS

When cows and other grass-eating farm animals fart, they release methane, which they produce as they digest. In addition, some farmers spray human-made fertilizers onto crops to give them the nutrient nitrogen. When microorganisms in soil feed on the nitrogen, they release nitrous oxide.

WARMING OCEANS

Water expands as it gets warmer, so sea levels are rising. Since 1880, oceans have risen up the shore by 21 to 24 cm (8 to 9 in), which is putting low-lying islands at risk. Warming oceans are also affecting sea animals such as corals. Many corals take food from algae that live inside their body and make their own food from sunlight. When seawater gets too warm, stressed corals push out their algae, leaving themselves starving.

MELTING ICE

Earth is losing 1.2 trillion tonnes (1.3 trillion US tons) of ice each year, as rising temperatures melt ice on mountains and at the poles. This is shrinking the habitats of ice-dwelling animals (see page 56). It is also reducing the fresh water stored in glaciers, which are essential as a steady supply of drinking water for local people and animals. Melted land ice is trickling into oceans, worsening sea-level rise.

CHANGING WEATHER

Warmer air and oceans are speeding up the water cycle, which is—overall—increasing rainfall, storms, and flooding. However, some hot, dry regions are facing more droughts, which are long periods without rain. This is because, as evaporation speeds up, it dries out surface soil and plants, further reducing precipitation in these already dry places. Droughts raise the risk of wildfires, which spread quickly through dry vegetation.

The Solar System

**The Solar System is the Sun and all the objects in orbit around it.
These objects include eight planets, at least nine dwarf planets, more than 285 moons,
and billions of smaller rocky or icy objects such as asteroids and comets.**

INNER SOLAR SYSTEM

The closest planets to the Sun are Mercury, Venus, Earth, and Mars. Mercury orbits closest of all, around 57.9 million km (36 million miles) away. All the inner planets are made of rock, with a metal core. As the Solar System formed (see page 106), lighter, gassier materials were blown into the outer Solar System, where they formed the outer planets. The inner planets are smaller than the outer planets as there was less rock and metal to go around. The smallest is Mercury, just 4,880 km (3,032 miles) across, while the largest is Earth.

Apart from Earth, none of the inner planets is suitable for life. Mars has little atmosphere and little or no liquid water, both of which are needed for life. Billions of years ago, it probably had both, before the solar wind—a stream of charged particles from the Sun—stripped them away. Space probes are searching Mars for signs of ancient microorganisms. Mercury has almost no atmosphere, and its temperature reaches a life-unfriendly 427 °C (800 °F). Venus is even hotter and has a poisonous atmosphere of mostly carbon dioxide.

Due to their smaller mass and lower gravity, the inner planets have fewer moons than the outer planets. In fact, only Earth and Mars have moons. Mars has two small moons, called Phobos and Deimos.

ASTEROID BELT

The Asteroid Belt is a region where millions of rocky or metal objects orbit the Sun. As the Solar System formed, this rubble was prevented from pulling together, into a planet, by the immense gravity of Jupiter.

At 939 km (583 miles) wide, Ceres is the largest asteroid and the only one big enough to be called a dwarf planet. Like other dwarf planets, Ceres is large enough for its gravity to pull it into a ball shape, but not large enough to clear other large objects out of its orbit.

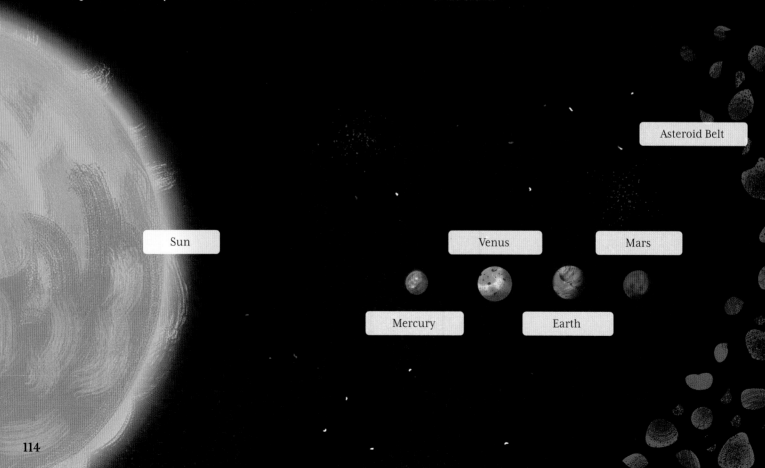

Sun

Asteroid Belt

Venus

Mars

Mercury

Earth

OUTER SOLAR SYSTEM

From nearest to farthest, the outer planets are Jupiter, Saturn, Uranus, and Neptune. The largest is Jupiter, which is 142,984 km (88,846 miles) wide. The smallest is Neptune, 49,528 km (30,775 miles) across, which is nearly four times wider than Earth. Unsurprisingly, these four planets are also known as the giant planets.

The outer planets are made of swirling liquid and gas, around a solid core of rock and metal. Jupiter and Saturn are mostly hydrogen and helium, which are gases at room temperature on Earth, so they are known as gas giants. Uranus and Neptune are mostly water, ammonia, and methane. They are known as ice giants because their materials were frozen when they formed, far from the Sun's heat.

All the outer planets have a ring system—made of orbiting chunks of rock, dust, and ice—and many known moons: Neptune has 14, Uranus 27, Jupiter 95, and Saturn 146. The moons are made of materials such as rock, ice, and metal.

Astronomers wonder if some of these moons may be suitable for life. For example, Saturn's largest moon, Titan, has an atmosphere and liquid water. Titan is so far from the Sun that its surface—at -179 °C (-290 °F)—is frozen. Titan's liquid water is in an ocean beneath its ice shell. This ocean may be suitable for microorganisms, but space probes have not yet discovered enough to be sure.

KUIPER BELT AND BEYOND

Beyond Neptune is a vast region of icy objects called the Kuiper Belt. Past this are yet more distant regions of Sun-orbiting objects: the Scattered Disk and Oort Cloud, which may extend to 30 trillion km (18.6 trillion miles) from the Sun. These regions are home to at least eight dwarf planets. At around 2,376 km (1,476 miles) across, the Kuiper Belt's Pluto is the largest discovered so far.

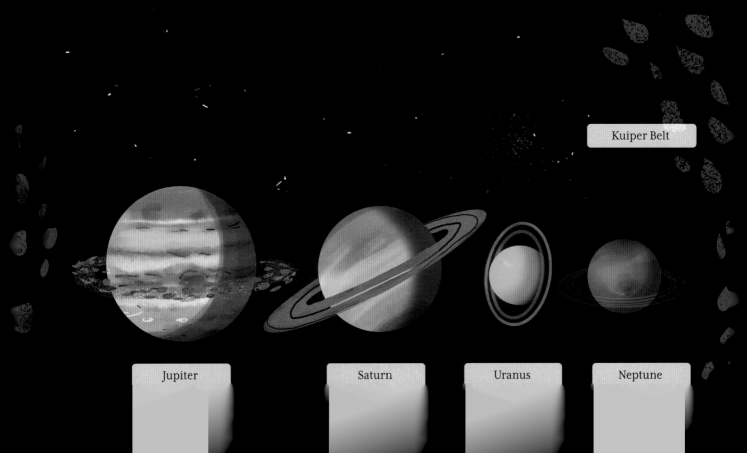

Kuiper Belt

Jupiter   Saturn   Uranus   Neptune

Stars and Galaxies

There are far too many stars to count, but astronomers estimate there are 1 septillion—1 followed by 24 zeros—in the Universe. Most stars are in large groups, called galaxies, along with gas, dust, and lots of planets.

STAR LIFE

A star is born when a cloud of hydrogen and helium gas collapses in on itself, forming a spinning sphere of matter. At the sphere's core, the nuclei of hydrogen atoms (see page 8) crash together, joining to form a bigger atom: helium. As they do, they release energy, making the star glow. The star is so hot that its gas becomes plasma (see page 18). Our Sun is around 15 million °C (27 million °F) at its core.

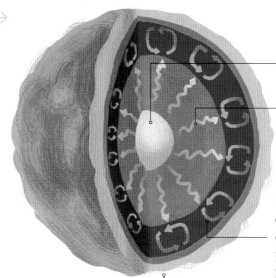

In a star's core, hydrogen nuclei fuse together, releasing energy in tiny packets called photons.

At first, photons travel outward by radiation, bouncing from atom to atom (see page 91).

In the less densely packed outer layer, photons travel by convection, as plumes of hot plasma rise to the surface (see page 91).

Photons stream into space from a star's surface. When photons from the Sun reach Earth, some can be felt as heat and seen as light.

STAR DEATH

When stars run out of hydrogen, they start to die. Huge stars—which can be up to 2.4 billion km (1.5 billion miles) wide—go through their hydrogen fast, in just a few million years. Then they explode in spectacular events called supernovas. Medium-sized stars like the Sun, which is around 1.4 million km (865,000 miles) across, die more quietly. The Sun has enough hydrogen for another 5 billion years, when it will swell, destroying the Solar System, then shrink and fade. Smaller stars, as little as 116,000 km (72,000 miles) across, simply fade.

A supernova (pictured) can leave behind a black hole: a region of space with such intense gravity that not even light can escape its pull.

Scientist Profile

NAME	Subrahmanyan Chandrasekhar
DATES	1910–95
NATIONALITY	Indian-American

BREAKTHROUGH
He studied how stars die when they use up their hydrogen, figuring out exactly how massive a star must be to explode as a supernova.

CONSTELLATIONS

A constellation is a group of stars that, when viewed from Earth, seem to make the shape of a person, animal, or object in the night sky. There are 88 official constellations. Many were named by ancient Greek astronomers after characters from their myths. Others, particularly those only visible south of the equator, were named after scientific instruments or animals.

The Orion constellation is named after a hunter from ancient Greek myths.

Our own galaxy, the Milky Way, is a spiral with at least 100 billion stars. The Sun is around 265 quadrillion km (165 quadrillion miles) from the galaxy's heart.

GALAXIES

There are around 2 trillion galaxies in the Universe. The smallest galaxies contain a few thousand stars, while the largest have up to 1 trillion, all held together by gravity. Galaxies have three main shapes: spiral, which are spinning disks with curving arms of thicker stars, gas, and dust; elliptical, which are the shape of a flattened ball; and irregular, which are galaxies that have been pulled out of shape by a collision or the gravity of another galaxy.

EXOPLANETS

Just like the Sun, most stars are orbited by planets. Planets outside our Solar System are called exoplanets. Astronomers estimate that there are at least 100 billion exoplanets in the Milky Way alone. Possibly, some of these planets are suitable for life, although we have no proof—yet—that any is actually home to life.

The nearest star to the Sun is Proxima Centauri, around 40 trillion km (25 trillion miles) away. It is orbited by at least two planets.

The Universe

Sceientists believe Universe began 13.8 billion years ago. In the first moment, the Universe started to expand from a tiny point. After 100 million years, the first stars appeared, followed by the first galaxies and planets.

THE VERY BEGINNING

We cannot know what—if anything—existed before the event that began the Universe. Space and time came into being when the Universe started to expand from a very hot, very dense point. After the first second, the Universe was already 200 trillion km (124 trillion miles) wide.

At first, there was no matter in the Universe. However, before the first second was over, tiny particles had formed, including protons, neutrons, and electrons (see page 8). It took around 380,000 years for these particles to join together as the first atoms. The earliest atoms were the lightest and simplest atoms: hydrogen and helium.

Gravity pulled clouds of hydrogen and helium gas into clumps, forming the first stars. No later than 200 million years after the start of the Universe, stars were clustering together as galaxies. It was inside stars—as atoms crashed in their cores or even as stars crashed into each other—that all the elements (see page 10) heavier than hydrogen and helium were made, when atoms fused together. When giant stars exploded as supernovae, the heavier elements were scattered far and wide. Once planet-building elements—such as iron, nickel, and silicon—were in existence, planets could form. The oldest known planets are 13 billion years old.

0 seconds: The Universe begins with an immense explosion.

0.000001 seconds: Protons, neutrons, and electrons form.

380,000 years: Atoms of hydrogen and helium form from protons, neutrons, and electrons.

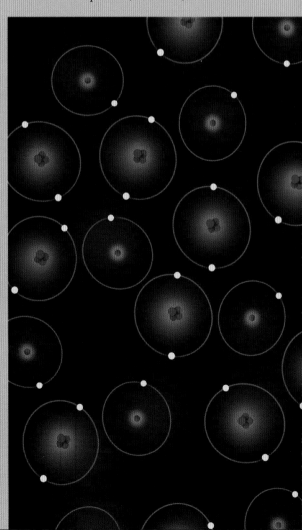

UNKNOWABLE UNIVERSE

The Universe has never stopped expanding. Today, the portion of the Universe we can see from Earth—known as the observable Universe—is 900 sextillion km (560 sextillion miles) wide. A sextillion has 21 zeros. The observable Universe is a ball-shaped region of space, with Earth at its middle. The electromagnetic radiation from the objects in this region has had time to reach Earth since the start of the Universe, allowing our eyes and telescopes to see them!

Light travels 9.46 trillion km (5.88 trillion miles) per year, a distance known as a light-year. You might think that we should only be able to see 13.8 billion light-years in every direction, since that is how much time has passed since the beginning. However, since everything in space is moving away from us as the Universe expands, the objects that gave off light 13.8 billion years ago have since moved farther away—to 46.5 billion light-years from us. This gives the observable Universe a diameter (side-to-side measurement) of twice that distance: 93 billion light-years— or 900 sextillion km (560 sextillion miles).

Scientist Profile

NAME	Stephen Hawking
DATES	1942–2018
NATIONALITY	British

BREAKTHROUGH
He created long equations that explain the history and structure of the Universe. He came to believe the—currently unprovable—theory that there are many similar universes, forming a multiverse.

Since we cannot see the whole Universe, we cannot know the full size of it—or if it continues forever. In future, light from distant galaxies will have had more time to travel, so you might think that further regions will become observable. However, those very distant regions are— incredibly—expanding away from us faster than the speed of light, so their light will never reach us.

100 million years: Stars are born in clouds of hydrogen and helium.

200 million years: Small galaxies appear, merging and growing larger over time.

800 million years: Planets form in the material spinning around newborn stars.

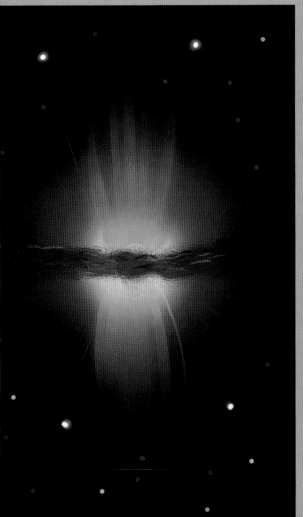

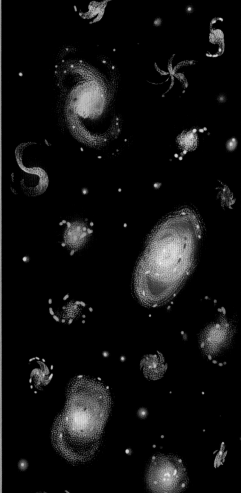

Questions and Answers

Hydrogen

Oganesson

Proton

Proton Neutron

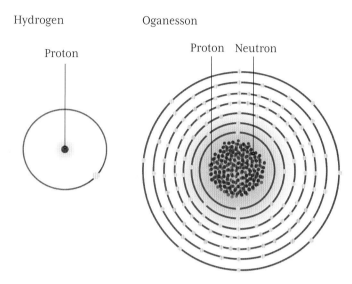

HOW HEAVY IS AN ATOM?

The mass (or "heaviness") of an atom is mainly made up of the mass of its protons and neutrons, since electrons have almost no mass. The lightest atom is hydrogen, which usually has just one proton and no neutron. Its mass is 0.0000000000000000000000017 grams. The heaviest atom is oganesson. An oganesson atom is around 294 times heavier than a hydrogen atom. It usually has 118 protons and 176 neutrons (which add up to 294).

WHICH LIVING THING IS THE BIGGEST?

The largest living thing may be a fungus: *Armillaria ostoyae*. One of these fungi, in a forest in Oregon, United States, is estimated to weigh 31,750 tonnes (35,000 US tons). Most of the fungus is underground, where it forms a mass of branching threads that spread for 9.1 sq km (3.5 sq miles). This fungus may be around 2,500 years old. Only the fungus's mushrooms are visible above ground, from summer to early winter.

Armillaria ostoyae mushrooms

White
blood
cell

Red
blood
cell

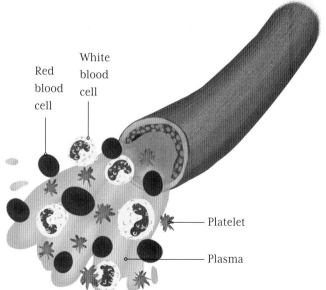

Platelet

Plasma

WHAT IS THE MOST COMMON CELL IN THE HUMAN BODY?

You have more red blood cells than any other type of cell. An adult has more than 20 trillion red blood cells, making up over two-thirds of their total cell count. These cells journey around the body in an adult's 4.5 to 5.5 liters (9.5 to 11.6 pints) of blood. Depending on their size, a child has less blood and fewer red blood cells: A 10-year-old may have half the adult amount.

WHEN WAS THE FIRST COMPUTER BUILT?

The first electronic digital computer was completed in 1945. It was called ENIAC (Electronic Numerical Integrator and Calculator). Like today's computers, it was powered by electricity and was digital, which means it worked with patterns of 0s and 1s, which turned off and on electric circuits. ENIAC was built for the United States Army and was 30 m (100 ft) long. The first personal computers, made in large numbers and small enough to sit on a desk, did not appear until 1971, with machines such as John Blankenbaker's Kenbak-1.

ENIAC

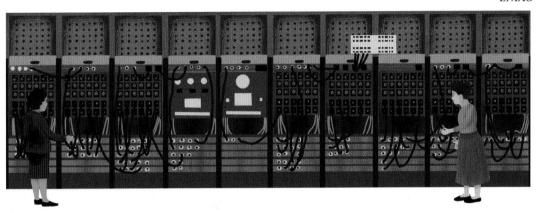

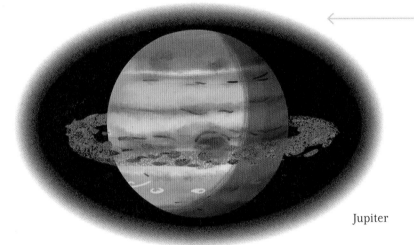

Jupiter

WHICH SOLAR SYSTEM PLANET IS THE LARGEST?

Jupiter is the largest planet in the Solar System. It is 142,984 km (88,846 miles) wide and has a mass nearly 318 times Earth's. In fact, Jupiter's mass is more than twice that of all the other Solar System planets put together.

WHY DO BALLS BOUNCE?

Balls bounce because, according to Isaac Newton's third law of motion, for every action there is an equal and opposite reaction. This means that, when the ball hits the ground, the ground exerts an equal force back onto the ball, making it shoot up. A ball made of a rigid material—such as china—would break, but a ball made of an elastic material does not: It squashes as it hits the ground, then snaps back into shape. Balls are often made of rubbers and other polymers. Their elasticity is caused by the fact that polymer chains easily stretch and bend.

Glossary

absorb
To take in or soak up.

alga (plural: algae)
A plantlike protist that usually lives in and around water, such as a seaweed.

amphibian
An animal that usually spends part of its life on land and part in water, such as a frog.

animal
A living thing that has many cells, feeds on other living things, and breathes oxygen.

antibiotic
A medication that is used to kill or damage bacteria.

archaeon (plural: archaea)
A tiny, simple living thing with one cell.

artery
A tube through which blood travels from the heart to the rest of the body.

asexual reproduction
A type of reproduction in which offspring are made by a single parent.

astronomer
A scientist who studies planets, stars, and space itself.

atmosphere
The gases surrounding a planet, moon, or other space object, held by its gravity.

atom
The smallest building block of matter. An atom has a central nucleus, containing particles called protons and neutrons, usually surrounded by one or more electrons.

axis
An imaginary line through the middle of a planet or other space object, around which the object rotates.

bacterium (plural: bacteria)
A tiny living thing with one cell. Some bacteria can cause disease.

biome
A widespread community of plants and animals that are suited to their region's climate.

bird
An animal with a beak, wings, and feathers.

blood vessel
A tube that carries blood around the body.

brittle
Hard, but easy to break or snap.

carbon dioxide
A substance made of carbon and oxygen atoms. Carbon dioxide is a gas at room temperature.

cell
The smallest working part of a living thing's body.

chemical bond
A strong attraction between atoms that enables them to join together as molecules. The bond often results from the sharing of electrons.

chemical reaction
A change that takes place when two or more substances combine to form a new substance or substances. The change involves the making and breaking of chemical bonds between atoms.

chromosome
A long, coiled molecule of deoxyribonucleic acid (DNA).

climate
The usual weather in a region over many years.

climate change
Long-term changes in Earth's temperature and weather. Since the 19th century, human activities have been the main cause of climate change, largely due to the burning of fossil fuels, which releases heat-trapping gases.

compound
A substance made of many identical molecules, each containing atoms of more than one element.

condensation
When a gas changes state into a liquid.

conduction
A process by which heat or electricity travels through a material. Heat energy travels through the vibrations and collisions between molecules or atoms. Electrical energy travels by the movement of electrons between atoms.

convection
A process by which heat travels through a flowing liquid or gas. Convection happens when there is a difference in temperature: The hot part of the liquid or gas rises, while the cooler part sinks.

core
The inner region of a planet, star, or other space object.

crust
The outer layer of a planet or moon.

dense
Tightly packed with molecules.

deoxyribonucleic acid (DNA)
A molecule found in cells that carries instructions for the growth, function, and reproduction of the body.

digest
To break down food into smaller, simpler parts.

dwarf planet
An object orbiting a star that is massive enough for its gravity to pull it into a ball-like shape, but is not massive enough to clear other objects out of its path.

electric charge
A property of electrons and protons, which are particles found in atoms.

electric current
A flow of electrically charged particles, usually electrons.

electromagnetic radiation
A type of energy that travels through space at the speed of light. This energy travels in packets called photons, which also—confusingly—behave like a wave of electric and magnetic force. Radiations are given different names depending on the amount of energy their photons carry, from low-energy radio waves, through microwaves, infrared, visible light, ultraviolet, and X-rays, to the highest-energy gamma rays.

electron
A particle found in atoms, outside the nucleus. An electron has a negative electric charge.

electron shell
An orbit that electrons follow around an atom's nucleus. An atom can have several shells, each at a different distance from the nucleus and each holding up to a certain number of electrons.

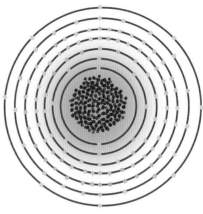

element
A material that cannot be broken down into simpler substances. An element is made up of identical atoms, each with the same number of protons in its nucleus. There are 118 known elements.

ellipse
An oval shape, like a stretched circle.

energy
The ability to exert a force or cause change.

enzyme
A substance that brings about change, such as breaking up food into simpler materials.

equator
An imaginary line drawn around a planet or star, halfway between its poles, dividing it into northern and southern halves.

eukaryote
A living thing made of a cell or many cells that have a central part called a nucleus. Animals, plants, fungi, and protists are eukaryotes.

evaporation
When a liquid changes state into a gas.

evolve
To change gradually over time.

extinction
When a species dies out.

fish
A water-living animal, usually with body parts called fins, that takes oxygen from the water using gills.

force
A push or pull that can make an object speed up, slow down, or change shape.

fossil fuel
Coal, oil, and natural gas are fossil fuels, which formed underground from the remains of dead plants and animals. Like all fuels, a fossil fuel can be burned to release energy in the form of light and heat.

fresh water
Unsalted water, such as in rivers, lakes, and ponds.

fungus (plural: fungi)
A living thing that usually feeds on decaying material.

galaxy
Thousands, millions, or trillions of stars, as well as planets, gas, and dust, all held together by gravity.

gas
A substance, such as air, that can move freely and has no fixed shape.

gene
A section of deoxyribonucleic acid (DNA) that contains a particular instruction.

generation
A group of people—or other living things—who are born at around the same time.

gill
An organ that takes oxygen from water.

gland
A body part that makes a substance for use in the body or for release.

glucose
A sugar that is used by animal and plant cells to make energy.

gravity
A force that pulls all objects toward each other. The greater an object's mass, the greater the pull of its gravity.

habitat
The natural home of an animal, plant, or other living thing.

helium
The second most common and second lightest atom in the Universe. Helium is a gas at room temperature.

hemisphere
Half of a sphere, such as a planet.

hydrogen
The most common and lightest atom in the Universe. Hydrogen is a gas at room temperature.

inheritance
The passing on of characteristics from parents to their offspring, through asexual or sexual reproduction.

insect
An invertebrate with six legs and a three-part body: head, thorax, and abdomen.

invertebrate
An animal without a backbone, such as a squid, spider, or insect.

isotope
One of two or more forms of the same element, with atoms that have the same number of protons in their nuclei but different numbers of neutrons.

kinetic energy
The energy of an object or particle that is moving.

liquid
A substance, such as water, that can flow to fit the shape of any container but takes up a particular amount of space.

lung
An organ that takes oxygen from air.

magnetism
A force caused by the movement of electric charges, which results in pulling and pushing forces between objects.

mammal
An animal that grows hair at some point in its life and feeds its young on milk. Humans are mammals.

mantle
A layer inside a planet or moon that lies between the core and crust.

mass
A measure of the amount of matter in an object; often called "weight."

matter
Anything that takes up space and has mass ("weight"). All ordinary matter is made of atoms. Matter has four forms: solid, liquid, gas, or plasma.

metal
A material that, at room temperature, is usually solid, hard, shiny, and bendy. Metals include iron, nickel, and gold.

microorganism
A living thing too tiny to be seen without a microscope.

molecule
A group of atoms that are chemically bonded to each other.

moon
A rounded object orbiting a planet.

multicellular
Made of many cells.

mycelium (plural: mycelia)
The rootlike body of a fungus, made of many branching threads.

neutron
A particle found in atoms, located inside the nucleus. A neutron has no electric charge.

nucleus
The central part of an atom; the part of a eukaryotic cell that contains deoxyribonucleic acid (DNA).

nutrient
A substance needed by a living thing's body for growth and health.

offspring
The young (or "babies") of an animal, plant, or other living thing.

orbit
The curved path of an object around a star or planet.

organ
A body part that does a particular job, such as the heart or brain.

organelle
A structure, found in cells, that has one or more jobs to do.

oxygen
The third most common atom in the Universe. Oxygen is a gas at room temperature. Found in air and water, it is needed by the cells of most living things so they can make energy.

particle
A tiny portion of matter.

photon
A particle that carries electromagnetic energy.

planet
An object orbiting a star that is massive enough for its gravity to pull it into a ball-like shape and to remove other large objects from its path.

plant
A living thing that makes its own food from sunlight.

plasma
A gas in which the atoms have ripped apart, losing electrons.

pollen
A powder made by flowers. It can fertilize other flowers of the same species, so they make seeds.

potential energy
Energy that is stored in an object, due to its materials, position, size, or shape.

predator
An animal that hunts other animals.

prokaryote
A simple living thing made of a single cell that does not have a nucleus. Bacteria and archaea are prokaryotes.

protist
A eukaryote that may be either multicellular or unicellular and is not an animal, plant, or fungus.

proton
A particle found in atoms, located inside the nucleus. A proton carries a positive electric charge.

radiation
Energy that travels through space at the speed of light.

radioactivity
A release of energy from the decay of the unstable nucleus of an atom.

radio wave
A low-energy form of electromagnetic radiation that can be used to carry information between communication devices such as phones and computers.

reproduction
The process by which living things make new living things, known as offspring.

reptile
An animal with a dry skin, covered in scales or larger plates called scutes, that usually lays eggs on land.

rigid
Unable to bend or change shape.

rock
A solid material made of a mixture of minerals, which are themselves made of elements such as oxygen and silicon.

room temperature
A comfortable indoor temperature.

sensor
A device that detects changes in its surroundings, such as light, heat, or sound.

sexual reproduction
A type of reproduction in which offspring are made by two parents.

Solar System
The Sun and all the objects, from planets to asteroids, that are orbiting it.

solid
A substance that takes up a particular amount of space and, usually, has a definite shape.

species
A group of living things that look similar and can reproduce together.

sphere
A ball-shaped object.

spore
A tiny, single-celled package—released by fungi, simple plants, and some protists—that can grow into a new fungus, plant, or protist.

star
A glowing ball of plasma, held together by its own gravity.

Sun
The star at the middle of our Solar System, around which Earth and the other planets orbit.

telescope
A device used to observe distant objects by detecting the light or other energy they give off or reflect.

tissue
A group of similar cells that work together.

unicellular
Made of one cell.

vein
A tube through which blood travels from the body to the heart.

vertebrate
An animal with a backbone: a fish, amphibian, reptile, bird, or mammal.

virus
A tiny package of material, which some scientists call living and others call non-living. It can reproduce only inside a living thing and can cause disease.

visible light
The portion of electromagnetic radiation that human eyes can see.

water
A substance made of oxygen and hydrogen atoms. Water is essential for life as we know it.

work
The use of force to move an object.

X-ray
A high-energy form of electromagnetic radiation that can travel through many materials.

Index